VOICES OF THE WISCONSIN PAST

YESTERDAY'S FUTURE

The
Twentieth Century Begins

MICHAEL E. STEVENS
Editor

STEVEN B. BURG
DAVID A. CHANG
REID A. PAUL
Assistant Editors

STATE HISTORICAL SOCIETY OF WISCONSIN
Madison: 1999

Yesterday's future

VOICES OF THE WISCONSIN PAST

Letters from the Front, 1898–1945

Women Remember the War, 1941–1945

Voices from Vietnam

Remembering the Holocaust

Yesterday's Future: The Twentieth Century Begins

LIBRARY OF CONGRESS CATALOGING-IN-PUBLICATION DATA
Yesterday's future : the twentieth century begins (Voices of the Wisconsin Past.)
Michael E. Stevens, editor.
Steven B. Burg, David A. Chang, Reid A. Paul, assistant editors.
Includes bibliographic references and index.

ISBN 0-87020-313-4 ISBN [paperbound]

1. Wisconsin—History—19th century.
2. Wisconsin—History—19th century Sources.
3. New Year—Social Aspects—Wisconsin—History.
4. Nineteen Hundred, A.D.
5. Twentieth Century.
I. Stevens, Michael E.
II. Burg, Steven B.
III. Chang, David A.
IV. Paul, Reid A.
V. State Historical Society of Wisconsin.
VI. Series.

F586.Y47 1999
977.5′041—dc21
99-25326
CIP

Contents

Introduction

Decades, centuries, millennia. Americans love to use these categories to classify time. Never mind that change does not take place in neat periods ending in zeroes; these words have become a shorthand for characterizing the past. Although long preoccupied with the future, Americans also have found that they cannot comfortably plot the trajectories of their lives without making comparisons to the past and the present. At the opening of the twentieth century, this tension between nostalgia and regret for the past and anticipation and anxiety about the future reached a fever pitch. While the century marker was a purely artificial line, it prompted people to stop and reflect about the kind of future they wanted. As Americans began thinking about new centuries as times of change, the process became a self-fulfilling prophecy, making the approach of a new century one more reason to embrace change for its own sake.

In the chapters that follow, readers can follow the ways that the men and women of Wisconsin experienced the approach of the twentieth century. The people of the state joined others from around the nation and celebrated the coming of the new century both in 1900 and in 1901. They reflected on America's accomplishments in the previous century and speculated on the changes they hoped would take place in the next hundred years. The items that appear here are taken from newspapers, magazines, and other printed material published in Wisconsin at the turn of the century. Newspapers of the era contained an interesting mix of original local writing, reprints of stories from in-state newspapers, and syndicated and reprinted material from out-of-state newspapers and magazines. Thus, while this book offers a perspective on what the people of Wisconsin read and what the state's editors published, it also tells a story that is national in scope. Together, these articles and essays offer a window on people's hopes and fears at a moment of great change.

Fascination with the future had been building throughout the last decade and a half of the nineteenth century. While the end of old centuries had been systematically marked as early as the close of the thirteenth century, the end of the nineteenth century saw interest in the future grow greater than ever before. The popularity of Edward Bellamy's utopian novel, *Looking Backward, 2000-1887,* took the nation by storm in 1888, selling more than a hundred thousand copies in the first two years after publication and becoming one of the bestsellers of the nineteenth century. Bellamy's novel told the story of Julian West, a young man from 1887 Boston who found himself mysteriously transported to the year 2000. The book depicted an America at the end of the twentieth century that had radically different social, political, and economic structures from those of the 1800s. Bellamy was not alone in speculating about the future. The novels of H. G. Wells, such as *The Time Machine* (1895) and *The War of the Worlds* (1898), speculated about the distant future and space and time travel. As the new century approached, Americans became increasingly conscious that they were living through a period of change and that the turn of the century would be an opportunity for reflection. The World's Columbian Exposition held in Chicago in 1893 focused interest on accomplishments and potential, past and future. At the exposition, Frederick Jackson Turner, the famous Wisconsin historian, delivered his paper, "The Significance of the Frontier in American History," which began with his observation that the closing of the frontier marked the end of an era.

Even before the start of the new era, publications throughout the nation began to use the phrase *twentieth century* as part of their titles to show that they were forward looking. Citizens in some communities formed twentieth-century clubs, and other writers began to attempt to forecast the future. Indeed, there were many reasons for Americans and Wisconsinites to be highly aware of change. The United States had ended the eighteenth century as a nation of five million souls scattered throughout sixteen states, largely along the Atlantic seaboard. During the nineteenth century, great social, economic, and technological changes shook the nation. Americans fought a great war that led to the abolition of slavery. Massive industrialization had changed the ways that people earned their livelihoods. Technological advances, such as the revolution in transportation, permitted one to cross the Atlantic in less than six days in 1900 compared to between seven weeks and three months a century before. By 1900, the federal union had grown to forty-five states, and its seventy-six million residents were spread out from the Atlantic to the Pacific. With the recent annexation of Hawaii and the acquisition of the Philippines and Puerto Rico in the Spanish-American War, America's territorial boundaries embraced the Caribbean and the far Pacific, and Americans struggled to become comfortable with their new status as an imperial power.

Wisconsin, too, had changed over the previous hundred years. In 1800, the land that would become known as Wisconsin was a remote part of the Indiana Territory, and the two largest sites of European settlement, Prairie du Chien and Green Bay, were isolated trade outposts with few permanent residents. In 1900, Wisconsin was a prosperous state with a mixed agricultural and industrial economy and a population of more than two million. Thus, amid great transformations, and at a time when Americans were highly attuned to the prospect of change, the turn of the century provided a reason to think about the future.

This book tells how Wisconsinites coped with these changes, first by celebrating, then by reflecting on the past, and finally by projecting a future for themselves. The first chapter opens with the debate about when the new century should be celebrated—whether 1900 or 1901. In Wisconsin, as in the rest of America and in most of Europe, the festivities were marked on the evening of December 31, 1900. However, the German kaiser decided to observe turn-of-the-century events on December 31, 1899, and Wisconsin, with its large German population, contained some citizens who chose to celebrate the earlier date. One wag suggested in the best Wisconsin tradition that the citizens of Milwaukee could resolve the problem by indulging themselves on both dates. Most people opted to observe the latter date, and men and women in Wisconsin used their creativity to celebrate in a variety of ways, ranging from pious church-going to late-night carousing in pubs and taverns.

Wisconsin suffered from a cold snap on the evening of December 31, 1900. In Milwaukee, two inches of snow fell during the day, followed by a temperature drop to two degrees below zero. Farther north, in Wausau the mercury dropped to twelve degrees below zero, and in Superior the temperature plummeted to a record-setting eighteen below. The cold weather kept many of the festivities indoors. Those not attending church or visiting taverns could keep themselves occupied by the many balls, banquets, and organized games that took place throughout the state, but the cold weather did not discourage all outdoor activities. On New Year's Day in Appleton, ten young men "wearing silk hats and huge chrysanthemums" rode around the city on a vehicle drawn by four horses. The convivial group sang out vigorously, sounded their horn, and stopped frequently at the homes of their friends and neighbors for a variety of refreshments—undoubtedly liquid and otherwise—to keep up their spirits. Newspapers, always interested in boosting their circulation, sought out stories about ways to celebrate the century, ranging from a newspaper contest in Superior to name the first baby born in the century to an interview with Betsy Hasbrouck, an Oshkosh woman who was born in the waning days of the eighteenth century and had lived to see the dawn of the twentieth.

New Year's Day festivities were not restricted to partying and communal gatherings. Newspaper editors, magazine publishers, and speech makers seized the opportunity for more cerebral speculations about the era that had just closed. Wisconsin, which had celebrated its fiftieth anniversary of statehood in 1898, got a head start on the retrospective reflections, but bragging about the state's and nation's accomplishments in the last century reached its height in 1900 and 1901.

Although Wisconsin residents gloried in the past, they paid even greater attention to the future. Americans looked with awe upon the great technological progress of the previous decades and speculated about the wonders that science and engineering would bring. Many writers offered strikingly accurate predictions, such as increased life expectancy through better medicine, central air conditioning, snowmobiles, air travel, and radio. One writer expected that in theaters of the future, "the lips of a remote actor or singer will be heard to utter words or music when seen to move." Others predicted advances in medical science: "The living body will to all medical purposes be transparent. Not only will it be possible for a physician to actually see a living, throbbing heart inside the chest, but he will be able to magnify and photograph any part of it." Other predictions were further from the mark. While many observers touted the future of "liquid air," others suggested that by 2001 humans would communicate with Martians and that most urban dwellers would travel to work by airship. Social change equally intrigued late-nineteenth-century prophets. Predictions ranged from the accurate, such as women's suffrage and the growth of the suburbs, to unfulfilled hopes for the admission of Nicaragua and Mexico to the union and free university education. A Janesville newspaper even speculated that once popular sports, such as baseball and bicycling, were to become passing fads. As an editorial in an Oshkosh paper asked, "How many things will the Twentieth century bring of which we may not even dream today? . . . Shall we reach the state of perfect toleration in human beliefs? Shall we reach the time when wars will be no more and eternal peace will reign over the nations of the earth?"

In the end, predictions depended on temperament and view of human nature. Some expected a glorious future, such as the writer who speculated, "If righteousness and justice and brotherly love shall go hand in hand with the advance of science, with the dissemination of knowledge and the development of nature's resources, then indeed it will be a glorious century." Other less optimistic souls pointed out that the new century was just a date on the calendar: "It will be the same old world, with the difference that the letter-heads will be dated 1901, up to 2000."

The writings produced while standing on the threshold of a new century provide an opportunity to examine the hopes and reflections of a generation of Americans, few of whom could have envisioned the amazing progress and unspeakable horrors that humans have realized in the twentieth century—from the miracle of organ transplants to the massive death and destruction wreaked in twentieth-century wars. It is unlikely that modern pundits could do better than their predecessors in their visions of the twenty-first century, but reviewing the thoughts and predictions of the past should serve as more than a warning about the limits of engaging in the imperfect art of prophecy. Some of the visions were mere speculations, but others provided important road maps for future progress. Technological advances, such as air travel, and social change, such as the battle for women's rights, stemmed from the hard work of individuals committed to seeing their dreams become reality. The dreams of any era, including our own, provide insight into the dreamers, their desires for the future, and the many paths considered but not taken.

*   *   *   *   *

The nearly one hundred articles and essays that appear in this book are taken from newspapers, magazines, and other materials printed in Wisconsin. Sixty percent of the pieces were written by state authors, while 20 percent were syndicated or reprinted items from out-of-state papers. The origin and authorship of the remaining 20 percent is unknown. The excerpts are taken from nearly forty separate newspapers and magazines originating in Wisconsin communities of all sizes, ranging from urban Milwaukee (population 285,315) to the Town of Dale in Outagamie County (population 1,273). In addition to articles from the mainstream press, this volume contains writings published in school newspapers, church bulletins, and periodicals aimed at a variety of special audiences such as German-language speakers, African Americans, farmers, and the hearing impaired. The six pieces taken from German-language papers are printed here in English translations, or in the original form if the item was written in English prior to publication in German.

The texts are printed as they appear in the originals, with the following exceptions. Spelling mistakes and typesetting errors have been silently corrected, with the exception of the spelling of personal names. Names of newspapers, names of ships, and book titles are set in italic type. Editorial insertions of words needed to clarify meaning appear in brackets. To distinguish these brackets from those supplied by the newspaper editor, all brackets in the original texts have been changed to parentheses. All omissions from the text of an article are noted with ellipses. Minor changes in punctuation have been made only when needed for clarity. The physical format of the newspapers has not been reproduced, consequently, headlines and subheads have not been included when they are used simply as typographical conventions and repeat information provided in the text.

*   *   *   *   *

Many people worked long and hard to bring this book into print. Steve Burg, David Chang, and Reid Paul, the volume's assistant editors, contributed in innumerable ways. The hard work, energy, and dedication that they gave to this project forecasts great success for them in their future endeavors. Ted Frantz and Kristen Foster helped with the original search for documents. Liberty Wollerman did excellent work in transcribing the original materials. Hope Hague and Madelon Kohler-Busch translated the German-language materials. Ellen Goldlust-Gingrich assisted with the copyediting. Jill Bremigan designed the cover of the book. Paul Hass provided his usual good counsel as this project moved from idea to book.

YESTERDAY'S FUTURE

The
Twentieth Century Begins

January 1901 calendar

Sun	Mon	Tue	Wed	Thu	Fri	Sat
		1	2	3	4	5
6	7	8	9	10	11	12
13	14	15	16	17	18	19
20	21	22	23	24	25	26
27	28	29	30	31		

Oconto County Reporter, *January 11, 1901.*

1

Greeting the New Century in Wisconsin

When Does the New Century Begin?

As the end of the year 1899 approached, people around the world began debating whether celebrations marking the arrival of the twentieth century should be held on January 1, 1900, or January 1, 1901. Fueling this controversy was a statement by Pope Leo XIII granting Catholic priests permission to celebrate special New Year's Eve midnight masses on December 31 of both 1899 and 1900. Ultimately, most of the Western world, with the notable exception of the German empire, decided to celebrate the start of the twentieth century on January 1, 1901. But the controversy continued, particularly in Wisconsin, with its large German population. The following piece from a Wisconsin German-language newspaper, published several days before the end of 1899, reminded readers that confusion over when to celebrate the new century was not a new problem.

(Appleton) Gegenwart, December 29, 1899

One hundred years ago in our old fatherland a vehement dispute erupted concerning whether the new year would begin on January 1, 1800, or on January 1, 1801. Schiller and Goethe were also drawn into this dispute, which merrymakers resolved by celebrating New Year's Eve twice—on December 31, 1799, and on December 31, 1800—with the then-customary punch and the obligatory waffles. This year, too, a lively discussion is in progress about when we should celebrate the beginning of the twentieth century. Many people think it will begin when we first write the number 1900 instead of 1899—that is to say on January 1, 1900, and this appears correct, as far as the eye is concerned. But others counter that the new century does not really begin until January 1, 1901.

Pope Leo recently decided this question for all Catholics with a pronouncement that the old century will end next December

31st. He probably couldn't have decided otherwise, since the calendar that takes Christ's birth as its beginning dates from the time of Charlemagne, and at that time the year 800 was considered the first year of the new century. Popes since then have repeatedly called for jubilee years, as did Pope Boniface VIII in the year 1500, with the additional mandate that the jubilee should be celebrated henceforth every hundred years. Peter the Great also held a similar opinion, since he chose the year 1700 for the beginning of the new Russian calendar. And now the German kaiser and Federal Council have also spoken in favor of this view. It is also effectively supported by the obvious concurrence between the new century's beginning and its new number. It would require the greatest effort to persuade most people that the old century had not yet ended when the number for the new century was already in use, since they are persuaded in this instance by the eye and not by mathematical calculations.

From a mathematical perspective, however, things look different. There is absolutely no doubt that there cannot be a full count of ten without including the number ten. If you want to have ten apples, you certainly need the tenth one, too. Seen in this way, the year 100 belongs to the first century, the year 200 to the second, and the year 1900 to the nineteenth. Mathematicians have always held this view. Littre's *Dictionary*, whose entries are based on consultation with authorities in the fields of science, states succinctly in its article "Century": "The present century began with the first day of 1801 and will end with the last day of the year 1900." The greatest contemporary English astronomer has also decided the matter similarly.

In any case, there is as little hope for agreement on this question as there was one hundred years ago, and the cleverest response would be to emulate Goethe and Schiller in celebrating the beginning of the new century twice: once on January 1, 1900, and again on January 1, 1901.

While the debate over the proper time to celebrate the century's end drew considerable popular interest and even elicited comments from prominent scholars and scientists, the controversy also attracted a number of passionate debaters determined to prove through complex analogies and elaborate mathematical computations the true date when the century ended. As the following short story that the *Milwaukee Sentinel* reprinted from the Cleveland *Plain Dealer* suggests, the debate over the century's end became increasingly a source of humor, and its most passionate participants were dismissed as crackpots.

Milwaukee Sentinel, January 3, 1901

It was a sunny December afternoon. The snow was fast disappearing. The eaves were monotonously dripping.

In the handsomely furnished parlor of the Kendall residence a young woman was watching a young man. He sat looking thoughtfully at the fireplace and she was looking anxiously at him.

"Come, Alfred," she said in a coaxing voice, "it will soon be over. Remember that I have prepared papa for the—the ordeal. You mustn't be so timid about it. Everything will have to be at a standstill, you know, until you have asked papa for my hand. He is in the library now. You couldn't have a better opportunity."

"Millie," said the young man without looking up, "let's elope!"

"Silly boy!" cried the young woman. "Don't sit there temporizing. Papa isn't a—a fiery dragon. You've told me over and over again that you'd go through fire and flood for me."

"Show me the fire and the flood," said the young man doggedly.

"And yet you fear to meet my own dear papa," said the girl reproachfully. "Why, just think of it, Alfred. You can have two new relatives for the asking."

The young man stiffened his shoulders.

"By Jove, I'll do it," he said. He set his jaw with a click as he arose. The girl clapped her hands.

"Bravo!" she cried. "Don't let your resolution cool. Just remember one thing. Fall in with papa's humor. Don't contradict him. Let him lead the conversation and wait for your opportunity. Then switch in quickly and have it over. It seems so funny that although you have been here so many times he has never seen you. But I've told him all about you. There, don't hesitate."

The young man had paused with his hand on the door knob.

"Wouldn't to-morrow do just as well?" he asked.

"No," she answered sharply. "March!" Then as he turned the knob she added, "Courage and success!"

Alfred Barnes found himself in the presence of Amos Kendall. The old gentleman did not look up as he entered. He was too deeply engrossed in a sheaf of papers on his desk to heed the newcomer's entrance. He was a grim old man with a short white mustache and a strange fashion of raising his white eyebrows and wrinkling his forehead. Alfred Barnes watched him for several minutes. Presently the old man looked up and caught sight of him.

"Ah," he said in a brusque tone, "so you have come. Take a seat. Yes, over here. Of course you know why I sent for you."

Alfred didn't know, but he remembered that he was not to contradict this terrible old man. So he only nodded as he took the seat that Millie's father pointed out. There was a brief silence.

Alfred grew a little nervous. Perhaps this was the opportunity that he was to embrace.

"Mr. Kendall," he said, "I have called—"

"I know all about it," interrupted the old man. "Let us have no preambles. I am open to conviction. No man can accuse me of being obstinate or unreasonable. If you can prove what you say that's quite enough for me. Go on."

Alfred started hard at the old man. What was he to prove? What sort of recommendation could Millie have given her father? He wished he had questioned her further.

"Mr. Kendall," he said with the boldest air he could muster up. "I am quite sure I can prove everything to your complete satisfaction. If it is merely a question of—of—"

"Time," cried the old man.

"Eh?" said the astonished Alfred as his rather prepossessing face reddened.

"It's a question of time, of course," said the old man. "You think you are right in the stand you have taken. You have set your heart on convincing me. I mean to prove you are wrong."

Alfred's heart sank.

"I don't think you can do that, sir," he said.

"Obstinate, of course," said the old man. "They always are. I've had a dozen here this week on the same errand."

"A dozen!" gasped Alfred. What a little deceiver Millie must be! But no, it couldn't be possible.

"There's one thing certain," said the old man; "and that is if you can't convince me you don't get a dollar of my money."

"I—I am not after you money, sir," said Alfred with dignity. "All I want is—"

"I guess you'd take it fast enough if you could get it," cried the terrible old man. "But you'll have to earn it first. When you do it will be time enough to talk about not wanting it."

"If you will permit me to say a few words about myself," began Alfred with renewed dignity, "I am sure I—"

"Confine yourself to the subject in hand," said the old man firmly. "My time is not entirely my own. There may be others here to-day on the same errand."

"The same errand!" murmured the dazed youth.

"Certainly," cried the old man. "Do you think you are the only one? We are wasting altogether too much time. Come, now, let me try the familiar argument of the clock on you. I want to see how you'll answer it. Do you see that clock on the mantel?"

Alfred looked at it carefully.

"I see a clock on the mantel," he finally said. He would have to humor this old man, and he would humor him in such a soothing way that perhaps his temper would soften.

"Go up and feel of it if you have any doubt about it," said the terrible old man. Whereupon Alfred gravely advanced to the mantel and carefully stroked the bronze case.

"I am quite positive it is a clock, sir," he said.

"Why don't you smell of it, too?" snorted the old man. Evidently the soothing process hadn't begun to take effect.

"I trust you will excuse the third test, sir," the young man cautiously said; "I have an unpleasant cold in my head."

"Is there a clock on that mantel, or isn't there?" cried the irascible old man.

"There is a clock on the mantel," said Alfred with much deliberation.

"And what time is it?"

"One minute to 1 o'clock, sir."

"To properly illustrate the point I mean to make," said the old man, "the clock will be in better shape after it strikes. Listen."

They both watched the dial of the timepiece with great intentness. A heavy silence fell upon the room. Presently it grew insupportable.

"Stopped, hasn't it?" inquired Alfred in respectful tones.

"What!" roared the old man. "Why, of course it has stopped! Confound these French clocks, there's no depending on them! Why didn't you tell me it had stopped?"

"You simply asked me to verify the fact that the clock existed," replied Alfred with dignity.

"You are a—a hairsplitter," cried the old man. "I understand how I'll have to deal with you. Kindly start the clock. When it strikes 1 we will know how to proceed."

Alfred did as requested and a moment later the clock struck 5.

The old man breathed hard.

"We will assume that the clock has just struck one," he said. "Let us further assume that the first minute of the hour just passed was the first minute of time. At the end of the first sixty minutes the clock of eternity struck one. Do you follow me?"

"I follow you very closely, sir," replied Alfred. "When the first sixty minutes of time had elapsed the French clock of eternity struck five—I mean one. But I don't see what this has to do—"

"Don't get nervous," cried the old man. "You'll see my meaning clear enough when I get through. The clock struck one. That meant that the first hour was up. When it strikes eight, eight hours will be up. Now take the clock of the years. When it strikes one the first year is up. When it strikes ten, ten years are up. When it strikes 1900, 1,900 years are up! What do you think of that?"

"I think that a clock that insisted upon striking 1,900," replied Alfred with a frank smile, "ought to be gagged."

The old man scowled at him and his face grew dark.

"Come, come," he growled, "no facetiousness. You can't hide your defeat in any such way. Doesn't this unanswerable argument satisfy you?"

"Satisfy me of what?" inquired Alfred, with a little tremor in his voice.

"Of what!" roared the old man.

Alfred realized that he must not contradict Millie's father.

"Y-yes, sir," he stammered, "I think it does. That is," he hastily added, "with limitations."

"Very well," said the old man, and his tone showed he was somewhat mollified.

"And now let me hear you define your own position."

Here was Alfred's opportunity.

"My position is an excellent one," he said, "and next January I am to be admitted to a partnership. The salary is unusually liberal and—"

"Hold on," cried the old man, "what are you giving me? I don't care a rap for your salary. No subterfuges. Stick to the business at hand. Convince me with arguments and don't go skylarking round Robin Hood's barn."

"I was trying to convince you," said Alfred. "I meant to show you that I can support—"

"Can you support any theories in contradiction to the one I have just shown you?" cried the old man.

"But I mean something more substantial than a theory," protested Alfred. "I meant that I can support your—"

Once more the old man interrupted him.

"My practical illustration, eh?" he cried. "Well, I didn't see how you could disprove of it. At the same time I have no doubt you'll go away calling me a crank."

"No, sir," protested Alfred.

"Yes, you will. All the others did. When a man stands up alone against the majority he is always either a fool or a crank. They called Galileo a crank, and all those other thingumbobs. I begin

Father Time takes a refreshing break from the debate over when the new century would begin. Milwaukee Sentinel, *December 26, 1899.*

to see that this interview will be productive of no good to either of us."

"But if you will only give me a chance to plead my cause, sir?" cried Alfred.

"Plead your cause! Why, confound it, man, you have been doing nothing else! I never saw such a long winded fellow. Come, this interview has gone far enough. Good day, sir." And the old man turned back to his desk.

Alfred arose with a helpless glance at Millie's father. He would make one more desperate attempt.

Then there was a rap at the door. A servant entered bearing a card. The old man took it.

"What's this!" he cried. Then he looked across at Alfred. "Aren't you Prof. Limpsy?"

"No," said Alfred.

"Didn't you come here to try to convince me that the new century did not begin on the first of January, 1900?"

"I never thought of such a thing, sir."

"But you came in at the very moment that I expected this man Limpsy."

"I can't help that," said Alfred.

"Well, what in thunder then are you here for?"

"I came, sir," said Alfred, with a firmness that surprised him, "to ask you for the hand of you daughter."

"Well, well, well!" cried the old man, and a sudden smile swept across his wrinkled face. "So you're the man, are you? Come here and shake hands. Millie has told me all about you. Of course she'll have her own way. Glad to know you. There, there, run along and tell the little girl it's all right."

A tall, cadaverous man entered the outer door as Alfred turned towards the parlor.

And as he smilingly closed the door behind him the happy young man heard the brisk wrangle of warring words.

Wisconsin Celebrates the New Century

Most Wisconsin residents marked the turn of the new century on the evening of Monday, December 31, 1900, with celebrations ranging from raucous parties and the discharge of firearms to genteel banquets and solemn religious services. The following four pieces capture how people in Milwaukee, Wausau, Kenosha, and Sheboygan broke with their daily routines to celebrate this once-in-a-lifetime event.

Milwaukee Sentinel, January 1, 1901

At 11:55 last night the City hall began to ring out the old year and it continued its incessant clanging for ten minutes, or until the New Year had crossed the threshold of Time, bringing the Twentieth century along in convoy.

Other bells took up the cue and swelled the grand chorus until it ranged out all over Milwaukee and into the suburbs, reinforced by steam whistles at the factories, and on locomotives in the yards and standing in front of trains in the stations. Then from the front of the Broadway armory volley after volley was fired by the members of Companies A and F. Women rushed into the streets from their homes and set off red fire, and other women and men came tumbling out of houses and homes cheering the new born year and wishing each other many returns of the day.

Men in the hotels and in the sample rooms joined in the joyous acclaim while others opened bottles of wine and drank bumpers to the little stranger. Factories in which the fires are usually banked with the close of the day, kept up steam last night and sounded their whistles in recognition of the birth of the New Year and the New Century. Notwithstanding this, the demonstration was neither as noisy nor as long continued as on many former occasions of the kind. This was due in a large measure to the number of entertainments in the clubs of the city, and the general observance of the fleeting moments between the old and the new as an occasion for religious services at the churches. At the former the guests paused between the measures of the dance to wish each other "A Happy New Year," and then "chased the glowing hours with flying feet" until Aurora began to awake the new born day. At the churches thousands of worshipers arose from bended knee to exchange the greeting and then quietly took their way homeward.

Never before, it may be said, has the birth of a new year been so generally celebrated in Milwaukee as was that of 1901, and never before was the celebration attended with so little noise. There was plenty of entertainment, but there was less reveling and the new year and the new century was heartily welcomed with more than the usual amount of good cheer, but it was extended in a more dignified manner.

The dying year was in the last stage of dissolution when the people began to turn out for the purpose of making the welkin of the incoming century ring with their demonstrations. The new era was preceded by and enveloped in a cold wave that made the home circle the most comfortable place to spend the hours of watching and waiting, and those people who did not attend the churches or enjoy the good fellowship of the club, stayed at home until the auspicious moment of welcome arrived across Time's threshold. Then they went into the open air and shouted their welcome. The hotel lobbies and the saloons were deserted except by the few strangers within our gates who had no where else to go.

There were services in all of the English speaking Catholic churches with the exception of Holy Rosary, and "watch meetings" at the Methodist churches. The other denominations, as a rule, held union services in which two or more congregations joined to keep up the vigil and welcome the new year and the new century.

At the Deutscher club, a Sylvester eve ball was given, and the members and their friends danced the old year out and the new year in with music's voluptuous swell leading them through the merry measures of the waltz. The Iroquois club members and their friends celebrated the anniversary of that institution and incidentally welcomed the new century and the new year across the threshold with a dancing party. The members of the Carlton club also gave a dancing party last evening which carried into the new born year. They will keep open house to-day.

At the Phoenix club the new year found the members sitting at the banquet table ready to drink to the health of the stranger as he came across Time's threshold.

At the Milwaukee club very few of the members were about the house last evening and nothing out of the ordinary took place. To-day the customary New Year lunch will be served from 11:30 until 2:30 o'clock, with lots of egg-nog to wash it down. The Old Settlers' club will also keep open house to-day, although their quarters were deserted last evening.

At the Bon Ami club a little group of congenial spirits assembled during the early evening hours and began bowling, but later the larger part of them went to St. John's cathedral and attended the religious services. To-day a New Year lunch with a punch bowl as an accessory will be provided and the club will keep open house to their friends.

The Millioki club house was brilliantly illuminated last evening, and the rooms were handsomely decorated with palms and flowers, while the members and their friends enjoyed an informal dancing party to music by Bach. To-day the club will keep open house with lots of good cheer and music sweet.

A dinner was given by R. W. Houghton at the Hotel Pfister last evening in honor of D. M. Place of Chicago. Covers were laid for sixteen. After the dinner those who participated joined with the Cotillion club at the Athaneum in dancing the old year out and the new year in.

"Whee-e-e," yelled David Norrell, on the tap of the clock when the new century was ushered in at the Central station last night. And in consideration of his having been "pinched" as 1901 began, he was released at daylight this morning, nothing more serious than drunkenness being charged against him.

"Here's a man with a record," said Patrolman Beale as he led Norrell into the station. "He'll be the first booking of the new century. Clarkson sent him in."

Just then a rifle was fired at the armory next door. Norrell pricked up his ears as he heard the announcement of the death of 1900, lifted his overcoat skirts like a ballet girl would her lingerie, whirled around on the tips of his toes and gave a soldier's salute with a yell, as the first stroke of 12 sounded from the city hall bell.

"Whee-e-e," as the clock struck, saved Norell a $5 fine on Wednesday.

The new century began with the thermometer at 2 degrees below zero and a chill wind from the northwest gave promise of colder weather to-day. There was snow yesterday, to a depth of over two inches, but it stopped falling before night, and was followed by a drop in the temperature. It was the coldest weather of the season, thus far, and for the first time during the winter the snow plows of the street railway were sent out to clear and sweep the tracks.

To accommodate the people who were kept out late for the purpose of attending the religious and other meetings, and also for the benefit of the revelers the Milwaukee Electric Railway & Light company operated its lines, urban and suburban, several hours later than is called for by the regular schedules.

Wausau Pilot, January 8, 1901

The 20th century was ushered into existence in Wausau with a good deal of rumpus—enough to awake slumbering humanity with such suddenness as to make many wonder whether hades had broken loose or the town had been attacked by a company of

Boers. There was clanging of bells, booming of cannons and blowing of horns. The morning dawned without a cloud to dim the lustre of Old Sol, but it was dreadfully cold, the thermometer indicating 12 degrees below zero. This extreme winter weather continued all day, notwithstanding there were many who donned their furs and tucked in their nobby turnouts, 'neath warm robes and enjoyed a New Year's sleighride. The large number of young folks at home from their different schools made the day a cheerful one to all, besides there was enough going on in the city to make the first day of the year and century an interesting one.

The rooms of the Young Men's Christian Association were kept open all day and they were visited by thousands of our citizens and were the favorite place for those seeking diversion and amusement. The whole afternoon was taken up in games and in the evening there was a most delightful entertainment.

3:15 P.M. Basketball game between teams from junior and intermediate classes. Juniors having had more practice were a match for intermediates in team play if not in size. The score being 12 to 11, in favor of intermediates. . . .

4:00 P.M. Baseball game between seniors and business men. The teams were unequal, six business men and eight seniors. The game was exciting and there was good playing on both sides. The game resulted in defeat of business men by a score of 21 to 12. . . .

7:30 P.M. There was a basketball game between two senior teams which were evenly matched.

At 8:30 P.M. A very entertaining program was commenced, in the hall on the upper floor, and the room was packed with an appreciative audience. The first on the program were a number of very fine selections on C. J. Winton's new phonograph. This is the finest instrument ever heard in the city and created much enthusiasm. E. M. James followed with a vocal solo which was rendered in his usual pleasing manner.

The feature of the occasion was the sleight-of-hand performance which was given by Phineas Pease, oldest son of Rev. Pease, of this city. It was announced that he would amuse those present for a short time, but none thought it would be more than an amateur exhibition of simple tricks. To everybody's surprise, the young man proved to be a wonder in this line. He appeared in full dress, was as easy as if in his own home, and the tricks which he performed, many of them, equal to those seen at the Opera House recently by the famous Durno. His part of the program lasted from a half to three-quarters of an hour, and has since been much talked about by those who were present. "Phineas," so we are told, has a splendid paraphernalia for giving entertainments of this kind.

Refreshments were served by the Ladies' Auxiliary during the afternoon and evening.

Owing to the severity of the weather the attendance at the watch night services, held in the M[ethodist] E[piscopal] church, was not as large as expected, but those who did attend felt amply repaid, the church was comfortably warm, the opening service of song helpful, and the two addresses, "A Review of the Past," by Rev. Adam Fawcett, and "The Church of the Coming Century," by Rev. S. N. Willson, proved instructive and inspiring. The meeting and year were closed with prayer. After hearty new Year's greetings all separated for their homes.

The Y.M.C.A. sent out a New Year's Greeting which was liberally distributed. On the same was the following:

"Among the good resolutions you may form at this season of the year, don't forget our work for men and boys. Then during the year nineteen hundred and one, let us earnestly and continuously work to coin our resolutions into deeds which shall live for good. With this thought, we wish you a better New Year."

On New Year's evening the Froshin Society gave their annual dancing party which was a successful affair in every way. The party took place at Woodmen's hall, refreshments being served in the Liederkranz hall, just opposite. The Froshins never fail of having a good time.

A very enjoyable party was given at Armory Hall, New Year's evening, by the young people. Notwithstanding the cold weather the party was largely attended.

Miss Imogene Harger gave a large number of her young friends a most delightful sleigh ride on New Year's evening.

The Record went back to the old custom of issuing an address on New Year's day.

Kenosha Evening News, January 2, 1901

It was a happy New Year's day in Kenosha and the new century was ushered in under the most auspicious circumstances. Notwithstanding the cold weather great crowds attended the services in the different churches. The two Catholic churches in the city at which midnight mass was celebrated, were packed to the doors with devout worshipers.

New Year's day was generally observed as a holiday. Business men closed their stores and enjoyed the first day of the year with their families at home.

The day was a gay one for society and many young people in the city kept open house.

The most enjoyable social event given for the welcome of the New Year was the dancing party given by Mr. and Mrs. F. J. Gottfredsen and Richard Welles at Central Music Hall. The hall never looked prettier. It was resplendent in decorations of flags and banners and the stage, on which the musicians sat, was elaborately banked with palms. In one corner of the hall a tiny pavilion had been placed, at which punch was served during the evening. The party was one of the largest ever given in the city, fully two hundred guests being in attendance. The music was furnished by Jacoby and Compton and it was so charming that nearly every dance was encored. At midnight dainty refreshments were served in the dining rooms, which were prettily decorated in green and gold.

When the hour of midnight marked the opening of the new century a rollicksome dance was in progress, but all the dancers stopped long enough to wish their friends a glad and happy New Year.

Many guests from other cities attended and the party was one of the most noted social events ever given in Kenosha.

The bachelor maids—Misses Calixta English, Loretta Toner, Cora White, Edna Holderness, Mabel Windsor, Lotta Hannahs and Marian Hale—made their first bow to Kenosha on Tuesday, when they were the hostesses at a charming New Year's reception at the home of Miss English on Park street. Fifty young men of the city were invited to partake of the pleasures of the day and the young ladies certainly made a brilliant entry into the social world of Kenosha.

In honor of the event the home of Miss English was prettily decorated with Christmas greens. The dining room was exceedingly pretty; about the sides of the room were hung festoons of smilax, while innumerable bachelor buttons were to be seen everywhere. On one side of the table a Christmas tree had been set up and on it was hung the different favors for the young men. The favors consisted of everything calculated to make glad the life of a bachelor. The table, at which ices were served during the afternoon, was done in pink and green.

The bachelor maids were assisted in entertaining by Miss Er-
rickson and Miss Madeline English, while the refreshments were
served by little Misses Margaret Eichelman, Inez White and Laura
Windsor.

New Year's day was a jolly one at the Y.M.C.A. building. The
rooms were open all day long and the bowling alleys, gymnasium
and game room had many guests during the day. In the afternoon
the Ladies' Auxiliary received the young gentlemen of the city in
the parlors on the second floor. Lemonade was served and a pleasant time is reported.

At Central Music Hall Tuesday evening occurred the first dance
of the year. It was given under the auspices of the A[ncient]
O[rder of] H[ibernians] and proved to be a charming event. The

WHi(W6)26196

"New Year's day was a jolly one at the Y.M.C.A. building"
in Kenosha, pictured here in 1898.

music was furnished by Compton's orchestra. A large crowd was in attendance and it was early morning before the strains of "Home, Sweet Home" marked the close of the first dance of 1901.

Another of the pleasant events of New Year's day was the card party given by Miss Ada Thomas at her home on Milwaukee avenue New Year's evening. The house was prettily decorated for the party and fifty friends of Miss Thomas enjoyed the evening with her. Cinch was the amusement for the evening and dainty prizes were given. At midnight the guests were served with dainty refreshments.

The Uniform Rank K[nights] of P[ythias], entertained a large number of their friends at a dancing party at Simmons' Hall on Tuesday evening to welcome the opening of the new century. The dance was a most enjoyable event. The large hall never looked prettier. It was decorated with a wealth of flags and palms and the emblems of the order were to be seen on all sides. Fully one hundred couples attended and enjoyed the hospitality of the Knights during the evening. The music was furnished by Jacoby's orchestra and dancing continued until early morning. There were many guests present from other cities to partake of the pleasures of the evening.

Sheboygan Telegram, January 2, 1901

Sheboygan gave a hearty welcome to the incoming new year and new century that was not less demonstrative than that of the larger cities when population and opportunities are considered. Bells were rung, fire arms discharged and other means employed to increase the din which is supposed to be the requisite concomitant of a reception to a new year, to say nothing of a new century. So far as Sheboygan was concerned, however, there was not an excess of this sort of thing. The whistle blowing and bell ringing were of short duration, there being just about enough of each to show that the occasion was properly appreciated. The discharging of firearms was somewhat sporadic, only a comparatively few apparently feeling that the duty of welcoming the new century really required that sort of thing. It is quite likely that a very considerable proportion of the population slept the old year out and the new year in.

In Sheboygan the only formal observances were at several of the churches. At the Methodist Episcopal church the services were

very interesting, embracing addresses by pastors on denominational progress, with sociability and the customary watch services.
Midnight masses were celebrated at the Catholic churches in ac-
cordance with the decree of the pope, the mass at Holy Name
church being followed by adoration lasting until noon yesterday.
Watch services were also held at the First Baptist and the German
Methodist churches. All of these services were well attended and
were doubtless profitable to the attendants.

Quite a number remained up celebrating the occasion in a way
that was perhaps anything but profitable to themselves. Many others jollied along until the stroke of the midnight hour, when they
resolved to turn over a new leaf in the year to come. Both of these
classes of celebrants will be the better pleased the least is said of
their observances. It may be remarked, however, that resolutions
taken under such circumstances are generally short lived and have
only the advantage of being suitable for use again a year after. . . .

Churches Celebrate the New Century

Many Catholics and Protestants observed the turn of the century by
attending religious services. The following accounts of an Episcopal
service in Oconomowoc, a Baptist service in Appleton, and an
interdenominational service in Oshkosh capture some of the ways that
Protestants marked the century's end as a time for spiritual reflection
and celebration.

(Oconomowoc) Zion Parish Paper, February, 1901.

The midnight service New Year's Eve was a wonderful success in
point of numbers and interest. It began at 11 o'clock with the
processional hymn, "A Few More Years Shall Roll," proceeding as
far as the Prayer of Humble Access, when a pause was made for
silent prayer, broken by the singing of a few of the old familiar
hymns, such as "Rock of Ages," "Nearer My God to Thee" and
"Days and Moments Swiftly Flying." Precisely at 12 the rector, rising first from his knees, opened the south sanctuary window just
as the bell in the big clock on the town tower began to strike the
last twelve strokes of the old century. Outside the moon shone
bright upon the lake locked in ice, across which through the clear,
crisp air that marked ten degrees below zero, the solemn tones
bore in upon the kneeling congregation. It was a solemn
moment—a hush and a pause that was truly dramatic. Turning to
his people the rector gave the New Year greeting and immediately

the century old bell in Zion tower rang out the old and in the new with a voice of cheer that met a glad response in every expectant heart. Then choir and congregation broke forth with the Doxology as they never sang it before and perhaps never will again this side of Eternity. Then followed the glad Te Deum by all the people as well as choir. After this the rector proceeded with the Communion service, the entire congregation that filled the church remaining throughout. By actual count, ninety-three persons communicated, nearly two-thirds of the whole number enrolled. Considering the midnight hour, the first intense cold weather, and the fact that all were residents the year round, it was a remarkable manifestation of interest. One devoted Churchwoman, who is 86 years old, was present at the sacrament.

The service was beautifully printed on heavy white paper with appropriate frontispiece "Special Services in Zion Church, Oconomowoc, Wisconsin." "The End of the Nineteenth Century and the Beginning of the Twentieth Century." The main portion of this order of service was the same as that used in St. James' Church, Chicago, whose rector, Rev. Dr. Stone, kindly offered the "form" to Zion Church, the rector's brother, Mr. T. M. Garrett, of Chicago, cheerfully bearing the expense of extra copy and all the work for our parish. An interesting feature of this souvenir was the page headed "Historic Notes," giving in paragraphs the principal events in the life of the parish from the first services in 1841 to the Consecration of the church in 1900. The names in full were given of all officers of the parish, guilds, teachers of the Sunday school and members of the choir. A page was also devoted to a list of all the former rectors with dates of incumbency. This pamphlet will be treasured in archives and referred to a hundred years hence when perhaps the same service will be said in Zion Church. A copy has been placed in the library of the Wisconsin State Historical Society and also in the Chicago Historical Society. Descendants of all present that night will rehearse with pride the fact that their ancestors attended that midnight service.

Appleton Crescent, January 4, 1901

The watch-night services held New Year's eve at the Baptist church by the Young People's Local Union was largely attended, the church being filled to its utmost capacity. A devotional service was led by the Rev. Ray C. Harker, the Rev. F. T. Rouse spoke interest-ingly on "The Promise of the Century," a musical and literary program was presented, and a very enjoyable social, with an apple feast followed. Two minutes before the midnight hour the con-gregation bowed in silent prayer, and as the hour struck and the new century dawned, the bells rang out, all voices were lifted in a song of praise, and after a short season of exchanging greetings the meeting adjourned.

The coming of the new century was also greeted by many pri-vate watch-night parties, and judging by the demonstrations many persons were awake to greet it. The night was a most beautiful one, cold and still, with a glorious moon bathing all in a flood of soft white light almost as bright as day. When the midnight hour struck, all the bells in the city pealed out joyfully, many whistles joined in, guns and anvils were fired, and for five minutes there was no lack of a "joyful noise." Soon, however, the watchers dis-persed to their homes, and the city again rested silently in the white light of the moon.

Oshkosh Daily Northwestern, January 2, 1901

The pastors of the First Baptist, First Presbyterian, Plymouth Con-gregational and First M[ethodist] E[piscopal] churches of this city hit upon a happy scheme when they arranged a watch-night ser-vice for the purpose of greeting the new year and century with proper religious zeal. The service Monday evening was one of much interest and the attendance was very large, taxing the ca-pacity of the church. The christian people of these four congre-gations and other friends were desirous of having some place where they might watch the old year out and the new century in and they gladly accepted the invitation to attend the services at the First Baptist church. Old and young were present.

The four pastors each conducted a portion of the service for an hour. Rev. S. H. Anderson of the First M. E. church addressed the gathering on the subject of "Watching Before God." Rev. George E. Farnam of the Plymouth Congregational church spoke on the subject of "The Enduement of the Spirit." Rev. G. D. Lind-say of the First Presbyterian church spoke on the subject of "The Leading of the Spirit," and Dr. James P. Abbott closed the evening with the subject of "Consecration of the Spirit." The pastors all

Stevens Point Journal, *January 2, 1901.*

spoke of the spontaneous desire they had to hold the services and they considered the occasion one of moment to every person present. They thought much good would come to the service and that many persons would as a result start the new year and century with renewed interest and a new faith in God. The services included the singing of hymns by the entire congregation. At eight o'clock the services began and it was shortly after midnight when the gathering was dismissed.

In December, 1900 Pope Leo XIII issued directions to Catholic priests around the world specifying the conduct of midnight masses for New Year's Eve. In the following circular letter sent to the parish priests in his diocese, Bishop Sebastian G. Messmer of Green Bay explains the procedures for Wisconsin Catholic churches celebrating masses on December 31, 1900.

Milwaukee Catholic Citizen, December 29, 1900

. . . Reverend Dear Sir: Last year Our Holy Father granted special privileges for the midnight hour of the 31st of December, 1899 and 1900. These privileges are the solemn exposition of the Blessed Sacrament, a high or low mass coram sso. and holy communion. The exposition and communion may take place, even if mass be not said. These privileges are again allowed in our parishes under the same conditions which we made in our circular of Dec. 15, 1899. By a recent decree of the Sacred Congregation of Indulgences the Holy Father allows a solemn exposition of the Blessed Sacrament from 12 o'clock p.m. (mid-night) to 12 o'clock m. (noon) of January 1, 1901, and grants a plenary indulgence to all the faithful, who having received the holy sacraments of confession and communion shall, during those twelve hours, spend one hour before the Blessed Sacrament exposed and there pray for the intentions of the Holy Father. The Sacred Congregation leaves it to the bishops to determine how long, in their dioceses, this solemn exposition shall last. Hence we ordain hereby, that it shall take place from 12 p.m. to 1 o'clock a.m. where the pastor considers it advisable, and from 6 o'clock a.m. to 12 m. wherever this can be conveniently done: but in any case there shall be at least one full hour's exposition wherever the priest will celebrate that day be it at home or in the mission or in both places. Thus the people will be given the opportunity needed of gaining the above indulgence. Desirous of having all the faithful of our diocese join in this great centenary devotion to Our Divine Lord and partake of the spiritual favors extended by Our Holy Father, we hereby grant to all our priests, having faculties to hear confessions, the power of absolving from all cases reserved to ourselves; this concession to hold from this date until next New Year's Day inclusive. We ordain moreover that in thanksgiving for the divine blessings bestowed on mankind during this ending century the hymn "Te Deum" or some other corresponding and appropriate hymn be sung before the midnight mass, and that before the benediction with the Blessed Sacrament after the mass, the Litany of the Holy Name of Jesus be sung or publically recited, in recognition of the supreme reign of Our Lord Jesus Christ and of our salvation in his Holy Name. . . .

Again I beg you to earnestly admonish your flock of their duty to conduct themselves in a truly Christian manner on these holy and extraordinary occasions, and to avoid most scrupulously everything unbecoming or giving rise to scandal. Let them be "holy nights." . . .

> New Year's Eve midnight masses attracted enthusiastic crowds that numbered in the thousands. The following two articles published in the *Milwaukee Catholic Citizen* offer different assessments of the behavior of the men and women who attended these services.

Milwaukee Catholic Citizen, January 5, 1901

The pastors in all the local Catholic churches who had services at midnight New Year's eve, were agreeably surprised at the large attendance and the good order and spirit of devotion which marked the large congregations. At St. John's cathedral pontifical high mass was sung by Archbishop Katzer at midnight. The church was crowded out into the lobby, the aisles being filled with people. Half an hour before the services began the church was filled and rarely has so large a congregation been seen at the cathedral. The services were very impressive and Father McDermott delivered an eloquent sermon. Fully a thousand persons received communion New Year's day.

At the Gesu church fully two thousand people filled the seats and crowded the aisles of the vast edifice at the New Year's midnight mass. Father Rosswinkel celebrated the mass and delivered a short New Year's greeting. The church was brilliantly illuminated.

All of the other churches were crowded at midnight mass.

Milwaukee Catholic Citizen, January 5, 1901

In all our great cities, more people were awake and moving at midnight, Dec. 31, 1900, than ever before. The midnight masses drew the masses. While there was much to edify in the devotion of these great crowds which packed our churches, there was enough, to the observation of the onlooker in the rear of the pews, to justify the reluctance of our pastors as towards the proposition of making the midnight mass an annual feature. Once per century will do.

> Perhaps the most unusual religious observance inspired by the coming of the new century was a gathering in Chicago described below. The event elicited comments from several Wisconsin papers.

(Janesville) Daily Gazette, December 27, 1900

Thirty-six persons from various parts of the United States who allege that by recent sign they have been led to believe that the second coming of Christ is at hand are assembling in convention here, watching, worshiping and praying that they may be in readiness to receive the robes of immortality. They are to remain in session until January 3 by which time they claim they expect to behold the object of their vigils.

Menasha Evening Breeze, December 28, 1900

A number of men have assembled at Chicago to await the second coming of Christ. They believe the time is near at hand. Why they have selected Chicago as the place at which He will make the first stop is a mystery. The scriptures do not even mention Chicago, and it has no resemblance to the new Jerusalem.

Marking the Beginning of a New Century

In addition to attending church services, Wisconsin residents sought to find unique ways to mark the beginning of the new century, while the editors of the state's newspapers sought to make the story of the new century vivid and interesting for their readers. Among those trying to find new ways of celebrating were a group of young men in Appleton who revived an old custom.

Appleton Daily Post, January 2, 1901

After ten or fifteen years or more of slumber, the good old custom of making New Year's calls was revived yesterday, and will probably hereafter be a permanent feature of New Year's day. Some of the ladies did not arrange to receive in time to let it be thoroughly known and callers were less numerous than they would otherwise have been, but as it was full many a man was welcomed, fed and sent on his way rejoicing. . . .

One party of ten young men, wearing silk hats and huge chrysanthemums, mounted upon the top of a tally-ho improvised from a hotel omnibus drawn by four horses, attracted great attention as they toured the town, with winding of horn and their New Year's salute:

> Happy, happy, happy,
> Happy ever be,
> Happy, happy, happy,
> Happy centuriee.

At each house where this tally-ho stopped a card was left headed "The Charge of the Light (because empty) Brigade. We have five minutes here for refreshments." Then came a pen and ink drawing of the tally-ho in full career, and finally the names of the callers, as follows: Charles Butterfly Boyd, Paul Van Eater Cary, Walter Lightfoot Conkey, Charles "Skat" Dickinson, Julian Skyscraper Eaton, William Halfgrown Holcomb, Edward Prevaricator Humphrey, Thomas Whirlwind Orbison, John Stevens, J(oke)r, Oliver Cooleddown Smith.

An Oshkosh couple marked the arrival of the twentieth century by holding a New Year's Eve party with a surprise conclusion. The Rev. G. E. Farnam who attended the gathering was the same minister who had delivered a sermon earlier in the evening at the four-church interdenominational service described on pages 19–20.

WHi(D28)45

A house party in Sturgeon Bay, January 20, 1901.

Menasha Evening Breeze, January 3, 1901

Mr. Ellis Roberts and Miss Margaret E. Fulley were united in marriage at the home of the bride's parents, Mr. and Mrs. T. E. Fulley, 29 Wright street, shortly after midnight of New Year's morning, Rev. G. E. Farnam of the Plymouth Congregational church performing the ceremony.

This simple announcement, however, does not tell of the surprise given the friends of the contracting parties, who had gathered in response to the following innocent appearing invitation:

"The Misses Fulley request your presence at the end of the century hours, 9:30 to 2 A.M."

Some thirty persons responded to this invitation and during all the early hours of New Year's eve, games and various parlor amusements were enjoyed by the young people. Between the hours of twelve and one o'clock, however, the bride to be quietly slipped away from the gathering, repaired to her chamber and donned her wedding dress. The dining room was then thrown open to the guests, who, though evidently surprised at the evidences for an elaborate repast, said nothing but took the places assigned. As they all stood at their chairs they bowed their heads as Rev. Mr. Farnam was apparently about to invoke the blessing. At this juncture Mr. Roberts and his bride to be, all unnoticed, took their positions at the table, which was but a step from the chamber door behind which they had been concealed. The minister's benediction commenced to sound oddly to the guests and one by one heads were raised and the truth dawned on them that they were witnessing a marriage. The affair was a complete surprise to all save the immediate relatives of the contracting parties. The wedding breakfast was a very elaborate affair, the table being trimmed with roses and carnations.

The bride is the elder daughter of Mr. and Mrs. T. E. Fulley, respected residents of Oshkosh. The groom is the only son of Mr. and Mrs. J. E. Roberts, 77 Polk street. He is in the employ of the Globe Printing company.

Young John Hood of Racine indulged in a relatively new hobby on New Year's Eve. Unfortunately, no image accompanied the news story.

Racine Daily Journal, January 3, 1901

John Hood, a West Side boy, is rapidly rising to the top of the ladder as a photographer of views, both in and outside of homes and other buildings. Mr. Hood has the distinction of taking the only photograph at the minute and hour that the old year died and the Twentieth century came in. It was taken in the tower of St. Luke's church and is a picture of George Shurr manipulating the keys of the chime of bells that rang out the old and welcomed the new. The photograph was taken by a flash light and Mr. Hood believes it will develop into a good one and he will name it: "St. Luke's Chimes Twentieth Century Photograph."

> While the new century inspired John Hood to capture the moment with photography, the excitement of the new century led John Loenis, a fourth-grade student at what is now Martin Luther King Jr. School in Milwaukee, to write a poem.

(Milwaukee) Excelsior, January, 1901

> The twentieth century has begun,
> With the year of 1901.
> We begin the year in school,
> Till June when we are free from rule.
> Then comes July the Fourth,
> And Thanksgiving Day, of course,
> Now comes Christmas with Santa Claus,
> And then—a little pause,
> And the New Year is here.

> John Rupple decided to mark the new century by gathering pledges to close on Sundays from businesses and saloons in the rural Outagamie County communities of Medina and Dale.

Dale Recorder, January 5, 1901

Since the Gregorian calendar was adopted by mankind the custom of forming new resolutions on the first of the year has been in vogue, and with the dawn of a new year and a new century many of our citizens were busy at this work.

"My last cigar" or "my last drink" was heard on every side. But there was one resolution made which did not pertain to "swearing off" from either of these habits. Its keynote is Reform and it was made by Mr. John Rupple of Medina. He resolved to bring about the closing of the saloons and that of the stores and other places of business, on the Sabbath Day, as is required by the laws of Wisconsin. Accordingly, bright and early New Year's morning Mr.

Rupple started on his canvass of the saloons and stores in Medina and here. From all he exacted a promise to close their places of business. The merchants gave theirs cheerfully, as it will give them a chance to enjoy a day of rest in the family circle and thus enable them to become better acquainted with their family. The saloon-keepers although not over anxious to suspend business on Sunday, their greatest business day, may after all comply with the wish of the community. "They will either close willingly or be compelled to by process of law, but close they must" Mr. Rupple is quoted as saying. We doubt the necessity of compulsion and rather think all will close of their own accord.

As a result of Mr. Rupple's call on the Wason Bros., a card in their window announces that the store will be closed Sundays except during the hours of 8 to 9:30 in the morning and from 4 to 5:15 in the afternoon; for the receiving and distribution of mail-matter. The other merchants and saloon-keepers who have signi-fied their intention [to remain] closed are:

WHi(V22)1250

John Rupple of Medina wanted saloons, such as this one in turn-of-the-century Black River Falls, to close on Sundays in the new century.

R. W. Sommer, General merchandise.
Drews & Bullinger, General merchandise.
E. D. Bacon, General merchandise.
Fred Jungman, Saloon.
T. D. Hall, Druggist.
Wm. H. Heuer, Furniture.
G. A. Bock, Hardware. (has always closed)
F. Saenger, Barber. (1/2 day from noon.)
Mr. Weiher it is said will close his saloon if the others do.

> Wisconsin's high society took the arrival of the new century as an
> opportunity to host lavish parties, such as this elaborate military ball
> held in Manitowoc on New Year's Eve.

Manitowoc Daily Herald, January 2, 1901

If all the world loves a lover, every woman loves a soldier. The
picture of beauty leaning upon chivalry and strength has found a
warm response in the human heart since time was. There is something in a soldier's uniform that is too attractive for woman to
resist and she would rather dance with a lance corporal with a
single chevron, than to lead the grand march with a chief executive at the national inaugural ball. Thus it is that the annual
military ball is ever an event of social prominence in Manitowoc
and while in other years the function has consummated a flattering success, never has it achieved the grandeur of the year of 1900.

Monday evening witnessed the third annual of Co. H., Second
Regt. W[isconsin] N[ational] G[uard] at Turner hall and elaborate preparations for the event which voiced happy anticipations
proved to be a sure prophecy of the reality as it was revealed in
the attendance and in the unaffected pleasure of the occasion.
Fully 175 couples yielded to the attraction of Terpischore, whose
wand was waved by Bieling's orchestra in a most delightful program of inspiring music. The scene presented was artistic beauty,
the decoration of the hall being a feature of the evening that
aroused the admiration of all. The red, white and blue constituted
the color scheme in effect and in the history of local society affairs
the elegance and beauty of the decoration has never been
equaled. The stage was draped in large flags, affording a screen
which hid from view the forbidding aspect of the scenery and
throughout the hall the bare walls were transformed to a view
pleasing to the eye. The supporting pillars to the gallery in a covering of white found a graceful beauty in the creativeness of the

decorator's art, shields of various colored paper being attached. Miniature umbrellas of red, white and blue, suspended from, and ladders of small patterns in the same colors, leading to the ceiling gave the finishing touches to an artistic scene. The electrical display was on a more extensive plan than ever attempted and was the crowning success of the evening's charm, extending a brightness to the lavish decorations. A large shield of lights fitted in colored globes of national colors, occupied a setting at the entrance of the hall, a star in similar arrangement centered in the ceiling and on the stage a collection of incandescent lamps forming the figures 1900, cast a mellowed light that reflected the greatest happiness of the participants.

It was shortly before 10 o'clock when the first number on the program was called and the zest with which the participants entered into the enjoyment forecast the most pleasant sociability. Special music had been prepared and under the direction of Prof. George Urban, the musicians rendered the selections in a manner that was highly appreciable and happy. At 12 o'clock supper was served in the basement and here the decoration scheme was also carried out. The spread was of excellent viands and was served by Caterer Hobert and assistants in the usual complete manner. Dancing was again resumed and until the sun's rays peeped in at the east windows, the revelry of the night continued. With the tolling of the midnight hour, denoting the birth of the New Year, and century, pandemonium broke loose and the informality which characterized the entire party gave license to hilarity that was marked for many minutes. University students home for the holidays and present at the ball, made the welkin ring, others adding voice to the din and greeting the new cycle of time with pronounced acclaim. The bugle blowed taps to the departing year and a welcoming reveille to the new.

The assemblage was of gaiety and youth and the credit for the dressiness of the party belongs to the ladies, all of whom wore handsome gowns that gave the spectator a pleasure in viewing the scene as they circled about the hall, the colors blending like unto a gorgeous and ever changing rainbow. To Sergt. F. J. Trost is due the success of the affair in the artistic and beautiful decorations and this was attested in the many compliments showered upon him. The committee on arrangement consisting of Capt. Knudson, Lieut. Stahl, Sergts. Mahnke and Ohde and Privates Mueller and Hagen had performed their work in conscientious and detailed precision and fulfilled the purposes of their office.

As a spectacle the military ball was an undoubted success and as a social event it takes its place with the notable occasions of the last year of the century and stands among the banner events of Manitowoc's social life. . . .

> The well-to-do could also celebrate with a fancy meal, such as this grand banquet offered by the Hotel Englebright in Ripon.

Ripon Advance Press, January 3, 1901

Including the dancing party supper guests, two hundred and thirty-five persons were served at Hotel Englebright on New Year's day. The dinner menu follows:

Caviar-Tartines.
Baltimore Oysters.
Celery.
Chicken, Gumbo. Consomme, Barigoule.
Sliced Cucumbers. Lettuce. Olives.
Broiled Columbia River Salmon, Maitre d'Hotel.
Potatoes, Rietz.
Scallops, Saute a'la Puree-Verte.
Larded Fillet of Beef, Mushrooms.
Diamond Back Terrapin, Maryland Style.
Prime Roast Beef, Natural.
Mashed Potatoes. String Beans.
Roast Suckling Pig, Fried Apples.
Asparagus on Toast. Green Peas.
Roast Young Turkey, Cranberry Sauce.
Cardinal Punch.
Braised Mallard Duck, Chasseur.
Boned Capon en Aspic. Crab Salad.
English Plum Pudding, Brandy Sauce.
Home Made Mince Pie. Lemon Meringue Pie.
Strawberry Ice Cream. Wine Jelly.
Fancy Assorted Cake. Mixed Nuts.
Oranges. Grapes.
Bananas. Apples.
Cheese: American. Edam.
Water Crackers.
Tea. Coffee. Milk.

WHi(X3)52131

The Hotel Englebright, Ripon, about 1915,
site of a lavish new century feast.

Newspapers sought to develop innovative stories to tap their readers'
interest in the new century. The two pieces below detail a contest
launched by the *Superior Evening Telegram* that lasted for almost three
weeks into the new century. The name selected by Johnson's labor union
was in honor of George W. Childs, whose donation of ten thousand
dollars helped establish a home in Colorado Springs for retired
members of the typographical union.

Superior Evening Telegram, January 2, 1901

What Shall We Name Century's First Baby?

W. H. Johnson of 1227 John avenue propounds this question
to all Superiorites. Mr. Johnson, Jr., is the first twentieth century
baby to arrive in this city, having been born just after midnight
New Year's morning.

Mr. Johnson is foreman of the *Evening Telegram* and if the reader
should notice any mistakes this evening he will of course overlook

them. As the first twentieth century baby to arrive in the city the matter of an appropriate name is not to be lightly thought of. The problem of an appropriate name was laid before the *Evening Telegram* by Mr. Johnson and with his consent it passes the question to the whole city.

The name must fit the boy and the occasion. Possibly some already established cognomen will be found which suits the case at hand or it may be that someone will make a name that will be just right.

The *Evening Telegram* will receive all suggestions and it hopes that there will be thousands of them. Address all suggestions: A Name For The Boy. Care *Evening Telegram*, West Superior, Wisconsin.

In Minneapolis the first baby of the twentieth century was a girl and the *Minneapolis Journal* has likewise undertaken to name it.

Superior Evening Telegram, January 19, 1901

The first baby born in Superior this century will bear the name Childs Alpha Johnson. This has been decided upon by Mr. and Mrs. W. H. Johnson after a good deal of deliberation. Childs is the name selected by the Trades and Labor Assembly and was immediately agreed to by Mr. Johnson. Alpha was the most popular among the names sent in to the *Evening Telegram* office and is considered very appropriate, the first letter in the Greek alphabet and in English means the beginning.

The christening will be public, at St. Albans church, but it has not been decided just when it will take place. Mrs. Johnson is in poor health at present and the date of the christening will depend on her recovery.

Baby Lundeen, down in Minneapolis, will go through life with the name Alpha Twencentia Minnea Lundeen. This makes a combination which covers all the features in the case. Alpha, the beginning, Twencentia, the Twentieth century, and Minnea an abbreviation for Minneapolis.

Several Wisconsin newspapers ran new-century feature stories in which they interviewed local people who had been born in the eighteenth century. In the following example, a reporter from the *Daily Northwestern* visited one-hundred-year old Betsy Hasbrouck of Oshkosh.

Oshkosh Daily Northwestern, January 5, 1901

Born in the last year of the eighteenth century and still living in this the opening week of the Twentieth century, Mrs. Betsy Hasbrouck who lives with her son, Matt Hasbrouck, on Ninth street, claims the distinction of having lived in three centuries.

"I don't feel any older than I did twenty years ago," said Mrs. Hasbrouck, on New Year's day, when a *Northwestern* reporter called to pay his respects to the most remarkable woman in the city on that day.

"If I could only see," said Mrs. Hasbrouck, "I would be perfectly happy. Of course I can see the shadow of my hand as it passes before my eyes and I can see the light from the windows, but I can't see faces nor tell who people are who call on me."

Mrs. Hasbrouck speaks entertainingly on nearly all subjects. She is happy to have lived to see the birth of a new century, and it is safe to say she was the proudest woman in Oshkosh on New Year's day. That her mind is perfectly active is evidenced by the ease with which she converses on various subjects. "If I could only forget some of the things that happened long ago," she said, "I might remember things that happened a month ago better than I do. I keep a-thinking of the old, old times, and when I try to remember things much more important that occurred a short time ago I cannot."

On the 20th of February, Mrs. Hasbrouck will be 101 years of age. A year ago she celebrated her hundredth birthday anniversary and received callers all day long. She occupied a chair like a queen on her throne and spoke and shook hands with her callers, who came in large numbers. It would have tired an ordinary person completely out, but Mrs. Hasbrouck said she was "as good as new" the next day.

This indicates that she does not fret or worry about the concerns of life the way some women do. It is one of the secrets of her longevity. She says also that she never took medicine to any extent and never drank strong tea or coffee. She is in excellent health, has no aches or pains, and the machinery of her life seems to be capable of several more years of wear. She takes a little exercise each day and during the summer makes it a point to take fresh air every day that it is possible to leave the house. . . .

Looking for something different from the standard accounts of sermons, banquets, and balls, a *Milwaukee Sentinel* reporter explored the city's streets and institutions and recorded his observations in the following piece, entitled "Incidents That Marked Dawn of the Century."

Milwaukee Sentinel, January 2, 1901

WRONGED WIFE SECURES PARDON FOR HER HUSBAND

Joseph Suchomski observed the dawn of the Twentieth Century by returning to his wife and family, whom a few months ago he deserted. This was made possible by his wife, whom he had left penniless, securing for him a pardon from Gov. Scofield, and early yesterday morning the doors of the House of Correction opened for him and Suchomski went forth a free man.

Suchomski was convicted of desertion in the Police court on Nov. 30, and was sentenced for nine months. He had told his wife before starting to begin his term in prison that if he only had a chance he would treat her as he should, and she at once set about to secure his release. She laid the case before Gov. Scofield and the pardon is the result. It arrived at the House of Correction late Monday night. Bright and early yesterday morning, Mrs. Suchomski, who had been informed, went to the county institution and met her husband at the door. A New Year's dinner like the wedding breakfast of years ago, marked the reuniting of the two and the pledging anew of the promise to "love and cherish forever."

FOUND SHELTER WITH THE DAWN OF THE CENTURY

The new century was literally wafted into the Home for the Friendless, for when the winds blow chill and bleak as they did on New Year's eve it is almost impossible to keep the draughty, ramshackle old house, in which for so many years a noble charity has been carried on, even fairly comfortable. A cold night means that someone shall stay up most of the time, keeping the coal stoves going and the water pipes from freezing and so it happened that the first thing that happened at the home was when Mrs. Schoonmaker, just as the bells were ringing at midnight, shook down the biggest heater. Two hours before that the last arrival of the year had drifted in—a forlorn girl who had lost her place in a Chicago laundry and had come back to Milwaukee in hope of getting other work to do. By the time she had been safely stowed away in a clean, comfortable bed the new century was almost on hand and it came in to find the good matron stirring up the fire.

"But you can't say," said Mrs. Schoonmaker, "that that was an incident. It was merely the regular, cold night event."

Even Men In Prison Greeted The New Year

The new century found every prisoner awake at the House of Correction and ready to greet its arrival. There is a rule in the institution that prisoners shall not communicate with each other and that while in their cells absolute silence must reign, but on such an auspicious occasion as the end of the nineteenth century discipline was relaxed and pandemonium held sway. The boys pounded on the bars of their cells with tin cups and wash basins and screamed themselves hoarse with joy. From the stroke of midnight to the chime that announced the first quarter of an hour in 1901 it was impossible to make oneself heard in the din and at length the guards had to go around and threaten dire things if the racket didn't calm down.

Strayed Pigeon Announces Arrival Of The Century

"One of my pigeons escaped from the coop on the stage Monday night," remarked Joe Murphy, the actor, "and I thought I had lost the bird. What was my astonishment on being awakened from a reverie, for I had not yet retired, by the sounding bell and blowing whistle, to discover my white winged dove, pecking away at my window trying to get into my room. The bird had followed me from the theater to the hotel. Now I take that as a pretty good omen for the new century, so far as I am concerned. At any rate, when I awoke this morning I felt as young and as chipper as I was thirty years ago."

Four Men Observed It With A Visit To Jail

Four men who were brought to the county jail at the same time opened the new century at that institution yesterday. Thomas Bailey was released from the jail at daybreak yesterday, after serving a term of fifteen days, before noon was "loaded" again, and within six hours was in the jail again. Joseph Wocher was chilled through by the cold which ushered the new century into Pigsville so went up to an acquaintance, it was charged, and tapped him lightly in the jaw. For that he is likely to spend the winter in the House of Corrections. Thomas Benson and Thomas Buyerns danced the old century out, and before the new one was fairly begun had given two of their friends bloody noses, the complaints say, and were arrested.

Happy Because His Operation Was Successful

Louis Collins, who had just successfully come through a trephining operation at Emergency hospital and who is finding conversation the most delightful thing in the world, began the new century by making an early round of the wards and stopping at every bed to wish its unfortunate patient a Happy New Year. There wasn't a more cheerful person in town than Louis, with his mended skull.

He Gets A Retainer While Bells Are Ringing

"What was my first experience with the new century?" repeated Senator Julius E. Roehr. "Let me see: I was at the Iroquois dance. Oh, yes. We were at supper when the bells rang out, and the most beautiful woman in the club house leaned over and said, 'Mr. Roehr, I want to retain you in a law suit. I will call and see you to-morrow or the next day and explain.'"

Hold A Jollification At Bed Of Blind Woman

The quaintest and most interesting event of the day at St. John's Home for the Aged occurred when shortly after breakfast those of the old ladies who could leave their room went to call upon Miss Hinton, who has seen all but nine years of the century just past. She is bed-ridden but there was no cheerier New Year celebrant in the city than this little old lady of ninety-one winters as bolstered up among the pillows she welcomed her fellow guests of the home.

Had A Sleigh Ride In Two Centuries

"That man's dead anxious to say he had a sleigh ride in two centuries," said a sidewalk spectator as he watched a horse laboriously drag a cutter down Grand avenue at midnight with a man and a woman as its occupants.

First Fire Alarm Was On Fool's Errand

The Fire department's first call of the new century was to put out the sun, not a fire. The red rays of Old Sol as he sank in the west shone on the steam from the South Bay street malt house of the American Malting company and the vapor which sifted out from the plant was illumined like the reflection on the smoke of a million dollar fire at midnight. Box 266 was pulled but after an investigation of the malt house Asst. Fire Chief Meminger decided that he would let the sun continue to shine.

A Century Joke That Did Not Succeed

"My first experience with the century," said Joseph Flanner, "came in the form of a messenger boy and a telegraphic message upon which there was 60 cents in charges. 'I don't want any dispatch that isn't prepaid,' I remarked to the boy. 'Open it and see what it is,' replied the boy, 'and then if you don't want it you don't have to.' I opened the dispatch and found that some one who signed the name 'Pearl,' and was sojourning in Michigan, wanted to borrow $20. It was a good joke, but it didn't work."

Orphans Greet The Arrival Of Century

It wasn't daylight when the biggest boy orphan at the Protestant asylum slipped out of his bed in the big dormitory and scampered down the corridor shouting: "Happy New Year." He woke all the other orphans and greetings flew thick and fast until breakfast time. But that was all that happened outside of the established routine.

Sparrows Also Were Noisy At Midnight

"My first line of vision in the new century rested on a scene somewhat novel," remarked J. M. Handley, the manager of the Bijou theater. "You know there are about 400 or 500 sparrows that roost out there in the pagoda in front of the house. They are attracted by the heat that passes out of the house when the doors are opened I suppose. They are to us what the geese were to Rome in the days of old. Well, last evening the electricians neglected to turn the arc lights off at the close of the entertainment, and when the city hall bell rang out at midnight, and the whistles sounded, and the National guardsmen began firing volleys over in the ar-

The Bijou Opera House, located on Second Street near Grand Avenue in Milwaukee, 1889.

WHi(X3)52127

mory, the sparrows awoke, and in the glare of the electrical lights they joined in the grand chorus of inharmonious sound and made such a racket that the policeman on the beat came running to see what was the trouble."

Reflections on the Opening of a New Century

In addition to being a time for celebration, the turning of the century was widely viewed as an occasion to reflect on the past and consider the prospects for the future.

Green Bay Semi-Weekly Gazette, January 2, 1901

To witness the opening of a new century is a privilege which is novel to all except a very few phenomenal veterans on the stage of life and even among these latter, few have recollection of the ushering in of the nineteenth century. These dividing lines between the centuries have a meaning that invites solemnity. These great measuring periods as they come and go are not to be lightly regarded. They cause one to look back and see the great achievements of the past and peer into the future and speculate as to what may be in store.

The occasion is one which is occupying considerable serious thought. In many cities of the country arrangements are being made for holding appropriate ceremonies in the nature of watch services. In observing the occasion Green Bay might look upon other cities of the country as New York, Philadelphia, Boston and other of the older cities do. She has seen centuries end and begin, before.

Some editorial writers looked to the new century with optimism as a time when the United States would realize its full glory as a powerful, prosperous nation.

Neillsville Times, December 27, 1900

A century is dawning! With what emotion man marks the flight of time! The wondrous tide of human progress, flowing higher ever, seems at each century's end to reach the limit, and little man, full of false estimates, swaggers with conscious pride in his achievements, and feels today that he is brother to omnipotence in godliness and potence, just as, in days of old Justinian, and farther back, when in Egyptian sandhills the chisel-blistered Ethiopes carved great tombs from solid rocks, in cocky, high conceit, man thought himself a highly finished product. And we today are full of pride, and glory in the illumined mastery of the age. The pace increases, life is more, and longer, men stop at nothing, have grown bolder, stronger, world conquerors, unplagued by mystery, unhampered by the shackles of the past, they have found means to master land and sea, and would now navigate the upper vast,—harness the lightning and the atmosphere, speed beneath cities like a demon flight, bring earth's remotest corners neighboring near, and yet shall outwing Milton's cone of night.

To Americans the century about to dawn promises to be full of grand achievement and magnificent national life. . . . We must raise a race of giants for the great task of government, and those giants must be pure and good as well as strong, for bad men should never have high place. Thus far for every emergency men have been found. We are in an optimistic mood, and believe that the right man will appear for every crisis, and that our beloved Republic by deed or by precept will yet work out the federation of the world.

> Not everyone viewed the arrival of the new century favorably. The following three pieces from newspapers in Sheboygan, Eau Claire, and Janesville expressed anxiety about the future. Dr. John Dowie, mentioned in the (Janesville) *Daily Gazette* article, was the founder of the Christian Catholic Church in Chicago and a healing evangelist. On New Year's Day, 1900, Dowie formed a utopian religious colony called Zion City, located in Illinois near the Wisconsin border.

Sheboygan Telegram, January 9, 1901

Now that the first thrill of exultation on entering a new century has passed away, not a few people are confessing to a sense of doubt as to whether the change is an altogether agreeable one, and to a sort of regret at the drawing of so broad a line in their lives. Those who are old, either in years or feeling, recoil timidly from the necessity of identifying themselves with a new era toward the glories of which they do not even hope to contribute anything, while, on the other hand, they dislike to couple themselves definitively with "the last century," a phrase that for so many years has had for all the world a moldy, ancestral sound, replete with the associations of semi-barbarism. The nineteenth century was all right, of course—while we were all in and of it; but now it is different. Some of us, and alas, how many! are still in and of that century, and the one just beginning has only the faintest of direct personal interest for us. It's a fine moment for the boys and girls, for those whose successes—and failures—are all before them, and no wonder they eagerly accept the prophesies of the great things to be done in the next hundred years. Some of them will do the great things, and a lot of them will at least see and profit by the doing, but there is consolation in the prospect for those who are only survivals from "the last century." The generation that was and the generation that is to be seem to stand strangely—and for the former, sadly—far apart, if you happen to have eyes for the distance.

(Eau Claire) Weekly Free Press, January 3, 1901

During the year about to close there have been 8275 murders in the United States, which is 2050 more than in 1899. The embezzlements during the closing year aggregated $4,502,134, which is more than double the aggregate sum—$2,218,373—that was embezzled in 1899. If there is not a good deal of swearing off" next Tuesday it will not be because the opening of the Twentieth century finds on this continent a people so far advanced on the march toward moral perfection that their conduct leaves no room for improvement.

(Janesville) Daily Gazette, January 3, 1901

The spirit of restlessness, that has developed rapidly during the past ten years, was never more pronounced in this country than at the opening of the new century. As a nation we seem to be going wild on fads of almost every description. One amusement

WHi(V2)1194

The old transportation and the new in turn-of-the century
Black River Falls. Bicycling became a fad in the 1890s,
and by the dawn of the new century some observers thought the
invention would quickly fade from popularity.

after another is adopted and thrown aside before it is fairly tested. A few years ago baseball was the national game. Today it is practically discarded. Bicycling followed as a craze, and last year millions of dollars were sunk in the manufacture of machines that could hardly be sold for the cost of the material in them. Just now it is golf and football. One too expensive and the other too dangerous to hold the bards for any protracted period. What the next amusement fad will be remains for some enterprising yankee to develop, and he is usually equal to the occasion.

What is true of games is equally true of religious and theological fads. The city of Boston, the old Puritan hub, is now the hotbed of Unitarianism and all sorts of peculiar dogmas. Almost every protestant church in the city prides itself on its liberality of faith and doctrine. The west always likes to lead, and so she is giving Boston several points along the line of religious fads. The latest is the city of Zion just out of Chicago, dedicated to Dowie, and his fanatical creed, and a great many intelligent people with wheels in their heads, are joining the Dowie ranks. Faith cure, Christian science, and other fads of this class, are likely to be eclipsed by the Zion movement.

Four years ago the country went crazy wild over the free silver fad and almost half the voting population expressed a belief that a fifty cent dollar was honest.

This spirit of restlessness suggests an element of danger, and prompts the question in the minds of many thoughtful people: Is the nation drifting away from the old landmarks toward a point where self government is endangered? The fanatic, be he religious or political, is an unsafe leader. France has been cursed with this kind of sentiment, ever since she became a republic, and it has always been, and is today, an open question as to whether the nation will long continue under its present form of government. Her weakness is, of course, socialism, but every fad of a political or religious character partakes of the same nature. A man or woman who can swallow some of the fads that are so popular in this country today, would reach the border land of socialism, and develop into full edged citizenship, without perspiring to get there.

What the country needs today more than any one thing is stability. There are some things that should be regarded as sacred, and one of them is the faith of the fathers. It may be a little irksome, but it is always reliable. It ought not to be possible in this intelligent age for faith cure, Christian science, Dowieism, and fads of this class to gain a foothold, and the fact that they do, is not a flattering comment.

Another thing that should be held sacred is national honor and honesty. Fanatical heresy, along this line, if it ever wins, means nothing less than national ruin.

Wisdom will prompt the nation as well as the individual to check and control the spirit of restlessness, so far as may be, in the interest of the best good.

> New Year's Day was often a time for resolutions to do better; the new century only accelerated this practice. In the next article, a Wausau writer questions the practice of making resolutions.

(Wausau) Philosopher, January, 1901

I note that there was an unusual activity in the resolution market. New Year's is the usual period for making agreements which are not intended to be kept, but with the advent of the century, which by the way, may have advented any one of two or three times before, there seems to have been an unusual impetus to this footless and fruitless pastime of little people. Good resolutions are the refuge of the small and the confessions of the weak. A man should do right or wrong without any agreement therefor with himself or anybody else. He should live as his heart dictates, and if that is wrong he should get it right. You cannot make morality the subject of contract, any more than you can regulate it by law. I see that the bishops of one of the churches announce with great gusto that they are going to spend a million dollars in the laudable enterprise of converting souls, by way of celebrating the twentieth century. That is well enough as far as the souls are concerned, but if these bishops can raise the enormous sum they have raised and can devote the tremendous energy they now pledge to this work, what have they to say for themselves for the years that have gone, and how are they to answer for the souls that went into eternity without waiting for the auspicious dawn of the twentieth century and the accumulation of the million dollar sinking fund. God has no anniversaries and I do not observe that the sun shines any brighter, or the north wind blows any balmier with the dawn of the new century than it did before. Mind, I do not criticize the activity of the bishops,—God speed them in their work. What I am wondering about is why any more activity in the twentieth century than in the nineteenth. Surely there were enough souls in the nineteenth and, so far as I know, not being in authority, God's grace was quite as abundant. Let us do what we have to do the best we know how without reference to the calendar; the season, the day or the year. Then will the heart be glad and the life filled with rejoicing. The best New Years' resolution you can ever make is to resolve to make none and let every day be full of effort and leave to the spasmodics the little period that follows the usual moving day of the conscience.

2

Reflections on a Century of Progress

"The Most Wonderful Century in the History of the World"

The people of Wisconsin not only celebrated the opening of a new century but also paused to look back at the events of the preceding hundred years. Like their peers throughout the nation, Wisconsin newspaper writers and editors expressed pride that the United States had grown from a tiny and weak nation to a world power. They touted the wonders of the technical progress of the nineteenth century, judged that the century's tremendous social changes had made the world a better place, and looked to the future with optimism. The following three pieces offer snapshots of the way Wisconsin newspapers depicted nineteenth-century progress.

Appleton Daily Post, December 31, 1900

Today marks the closing of what has doubtless been the most wonderful century in the history of the world, in the way of material achievement. To realize what has been accomplished within that cycle of time, in the various fields of human activity, is well-nigh impossible and of which scarcely a hint can be offered in a newspaper article.

One hundred years ago, however, our own republic had its birth through much of sacrifice, tribulation and pain, but was still in its swaddling clothes, so to speak. It was yet an experiment, though one which gave to humanity bright promise. Now it is a mighty and beneficent actuality, surpassing in extent, power and, let us hope, in true magnificence, the most extravagant hopes of its founders. At the beginning of the century it consisted of sixteen states—only three more than the original number—four territories and the District of Columbia. Now it extends far beyond even the boundary of the oceans—for better or worse. Then the total population was

"Uncle Sam 1901 Looking Backward: 'My don't those old fashioned pictures make one look ridiculous!'" Dodgeville Sentinel, *December 28, 1900; (Oshkosh)* Daily Times, *December 30, 1900;* Milwaukee Journal, *January 2, 1901.*

5,308,483, or only a little more than twice that which Wisconsin contains at present. Then the annual receipts of the federal government were about $10,000,000—only enough to pay its necessary running expenses now for the minor fraction of a week. The total number of post offices was 903 and the postal revenue was $280,804, whereas now the former are numbered by many tens of thousands while the receipts and disbursements extend well into the millions. A century ago the immortal Jefferson had just been elected president to succeed John Adams, who was the successor of the first president and most justly renowned American patriot, George Washington. The Revolution was then only about half as far removed as the war of the rebellion is now and the majority of those who distinguished themselves in that great revolt were still in the service of their country. The establishment of a government "of the people, by the people and for the people" on the virgin soil of the western hemisphere has been an inestimable blessing not only to the posterity of its founders but to millions of the oppressed of other lands and whose coming hither has redounded in as great measure to the benefit of their adopted country as to their own. Nay, more. The American colonists not only fought their own battles to a successful issue but indirectly also the battles of the great bulk of the people of Great Britain as well, whereby representative and constitutional government was placed on quite a different and much higher plane in that country than it had ever occupied before. In fact, the crystallization of Republican principles into this sublime structure of government and its survival of the most crucial tests of permanency, so that it is now as firmly established as a nation can be, because resting upon the consent and abiding in the affections of all its people, has exerted a beneficent influence the wide world over. . . .

One of the most noteworthy facts incident to the century now about to pass into history is the marvelous development of labor-saving machinery, whereby the productive power of human hands has been increased to an incalculable extent in all branches of industry and the price of all manufactures has been correspondingly reduced to the consumer. Indeed, the economic conditions of the world have been repeatedly revolutionized by this means and the end is not yet, all of which is due to the inventive genius of Americans more than that of any other people, or one might safely say of all others. A hint or two will suggest the extraordinary progress which has been made in all directions. At the beginning of the century, wool, cotton and flax were spun and woven by hand and generally by each family to supply its own wants. Grain was cut by hand and threshed with a flail. And in the printing of books and newspapers the expansion of facilities has been at least quite as remarkable. In a word, at the opening of the century nearly all manufactures were the product of manual labor whereas now the human hand does little else than manipulate or guide machinery by which they are fashioned and at a small fractional part of the original cost.

During the period under consideration also, in a corresponding degree at least to the material advancement noted, has been the growth of educational facilities, especially in this country, in respect of common and intermediate schools and higher institutions of learning. Indeed, to the latter fact is due the great strides which have been made in the other direction. Christianity, too, has taken a firmer, deeper and more comprehensive, albeit gentler, hold of the world during the century, and to such an extent as this is true have the physical and intellectual achievements redounded to the greatest good of the greatest number of mankind. Without disparaging other forms of religion which have much that is commendatory, this system, after nineteen full centuries of test, stands par excellence as the world's exemplar. True its teachings have often been perverted and mistaken means have been employed for its propagation, but on the whole civilization has advanced or retrograded with Christianity. And whether one can accept its mysteries or not, as none can fathom them, no one can deny that if there were a universal and practical application of its philosophy, an ideal social state would supervene—when countless thousands would no longer mourn because of man's inhumanity to man.

But enough. The world is infinitely the better and richer because of the achievements of the nineteenth century and the new century opens auspiciously. Our wish is that so much of it as may be vouchsafed to our readers may contribute to their happiness.

Oshkosh Daily Northwestern, December 31, 1900

Tomorrow will open the Twentieth century. With today passes away the Nineteenth century, the most momentous in the world's history. To the happiness, comfort and enlightenment of the race

the Nineteenth century has contributed more than all the eighteen centuries preceding it. Over half of the first eighteen centuries of our era was wasted in warfare and devastation among
peoples and nations and between peoples of the same nation, in
cutting each other's throats, burning each other at the stake and
in other ways persecuting each other because they did not all believe alike in the manner of worshiping God. If perchance a great
discoverer made a great discovery, he was punished for his pains,
if not put to death, because such discovery was likely to in some
manner contravene the prevailing religious faith. The few notable
advances in science and utilities had to be kept secret for fear of
arousing the antipathy of the church. Massacre and misery, big-
otry and superstition were the ruling features of most of the christian era, up to the last two centuries, and it was not until the
Nineteenth century that the world seemed to have merged into
that toleration and liberal research that has made possible the
wonderful advancement of mankind in all the ways that promote
civilization and human happiness.

The Nineteenth century has given us all we see around us that
is today considered essential to our welfare. It has given us the
railway, the steamboat, the telegraph, the telephone, the electric
light, the electric motor, the Atlantic cable, the sewing machine,
the typewriter, the printing press, the bicycle, the automobile and
many other important conveniences of life too numerous to mention. In the scientific world the advancement has been on a par
with that achieved in the mechanical world. In astronomy, medicine, surgery, chemistry, photography and kindred fields of research, the most important discoveries have been made or those
previously made have been rendered of practical value. In the
engines of warfare there has been a complete revolution, with the
result that the more destructive have become the implements of
war the less frequent have wars become. The changes in our own
country during the century now closed have been marvelous. One
hundred years ago the United States was bounded on the north
by the great lakes, on the west by the Mississippi river, on the east
by the Atlantic and it did not reach the gulf. Today it stretches
from ocean to ocean and from the lakes to the gulf and into the
gulf and far across the Pacific into the islands of the sea, and far
north to the Arctic regions along [the] Bering sea. From a population of a little more than five millions in 1800, the United States

has grown to a population of over seventy-six millions in 1900. In 1800 the government expenses were less than twelve millions of dollars annually, and in 1900 they are over a billion dollars. In 1800 it cost 25 cents to send by mail what may now be sent for 2 cents. These are but a few items to indicate the wonderful progress of the past century in those things which go to ease the lot of man and make life richer in those comforts and enjoyments which are really the object of life. In fact the world did not begin to live, as we understand life today, until close to the present century. It was too wrapped up in its prejudices and false notions and narrow bigotries to afford time or opportunity for mental expansion.

But, judging from the marvelous achievements of the Nineteenth century, what may be expected of the Twentieth century? Not even the imagination may picture to us, for who in the Eighteenth century imagined the steam railway and the telegraph or believed we could harness the lighting to make artificial suns? How many things will the Twentieth century bring of which we may not even dream today? Shall we fly in the air like birds, or at least travel through the atmosphere by means of aerial navigation? Shall we find the elixir of life by which death will be but a matter of choice? Shall we harness the sun's rays as we have harnessed electricity and utilize them for heat and power, and to turn darkness into day? Shall we reach the state of perfect toleration in human beliefs? Shall we reach the time when wars will be no more and eternal peace will reign over the nations of the earth? Perhaps not all of these things will come to pass, but some of them may, and others of which we may now scarcely conceive. A glorious prospect spreads before us fortified by every incentive to further progress and discovery. And he who lives to scan the Twentieth century as it merges into the Twenty-first may look back with as startling comparisons as we now employ in speaking of the Nineteenth.

Green Bay Advocate, January 4, 1901

A comprehensive summary of the more important advances in law during the century just closed was chronicled in a paper read by Attorney F. C. Cady during the evening service, Sunday, of the Union Congregational church on the subject, "The Century's Progress in Law." In part Mr. Cady said:

Dueling has been legislated out of existence. At the beginning of the century men fought upon the slightest provocation. Lotteries can no longer exist except in violation of law. Lynchings are comparatively few, and those who take part in them are in danger of punishment. Piracy is ended. National controversies are being largely settled by arbitration.

The world is learning the lesson that war is never justifiable except as a means of securing peace. The century has revolutionized the treatment of the insane. The laws governing the rights of married women have felt the touch of progress. Formerly a woman's identity was merged in that of her husband. They became one, and in the eye of the law, that one was the husband. The vision of the law has cleared and in that clearer vision husband and wife are seen to stand together, with rights and privileges in most respects equal. The protection which the law has thrown around married women, however, is not confined to their social rights, but embraces their property rights as well. By her marriage no rights are now forfeited. She retains the titles and right of control of her personal property. The management and income of her real estate are hers. She may purchase, enjoy and sell all kinds of property as she will. Her separate estate cannot be interfered with by her husband. She may engage in business and her earnings are her own.

Perhaps the greatest step of progress in the law of this century has been the abolition of slavery. To those who have grown up in the last 30 years this will, perhaps, be thought incredible. One must be familiar with the struggle of the mighty opposing forces which lasted for more than 50 years to realize the significance of the proclamation of emancipation.

Imprisonment for debt has been done away with. The law has passed from a condition where a man's body could be held for his debts to one where this cannot only no longer be done but where his family cannot be deprived of certain articles and earnings belonging to him. Exemption laws may be abused—they are often—but in principle they are right.

Court methods have changed for the better, although some surprising things are still seen in justice courts if one gets far enough from Green Bay. Another progressive step is the comparative expedition with which matters in court are now disposed of. Some people still complain that courts are slow. It should not be forgotten that good work is inconsistent with too great dispatch. . . .

TO THE DYING CENTURY

Dying Century! a health
to thee! ☒ ☒ ☒
Take it to Eternity;
Tell the gods to whom
you go — ☒ ☒
Where the winds of
Heaven blow —
That you brought
me here, anon,
Heritage of tasks
undone; ☒ ☒
Robbed me of my
strength at noon;
Granted but a
single boom —
Yet that was Love.

Marion Thornton
Egbert

Oconto Falls Herald, *December 14, 1900.*

"The Blessings of Government"

The final years of the nineteenth century witnessed the rise of the
United States to an unprecedented level of international prominence,
and Wisconsin newspapers were caught up in the powerful wave of
patriotism that swept across America. In a hundred years, the United
States had prospered as it conquered a continent and built a powerful
government. Each of the following pieces offers a slightly different view
of the nation's history. The German-language *Buffalo County Republikaner
und Alma Blätter* praised the superiority of American ways, while a
Racine newspaper reflected on America's territorial expansion
from the Louisiana Purchase to efforts to suppress the nationalist
insurrection in the newly acquired Philippines.

(Alma) Buffalo County Republikaner und Alma Blätter,
January 1, 1901

A new century—the twentieth—is beginning! This news will be broadcast tonight at twelve midnight from the bronze mouths of the bells. We will be there as the world steps from one century into the next, and—a serious thought for young and old—when this event occurs again, nothing will remain of us; at most a mounded grave, perhaps held in honor by a distant relative, will mark the place where we were laid to rest.

And so the approaching New Year's Eve is doubly interesting and significant. Not only are we looking back on a bygone year, but on a bygone century, and truly, it is a magnificent picture that passes before our eyes, a picture of the most gigantic steps forward, a picture of improvements, of complete transformation and change.

In these one hundred years an unforeseen transformation in the life and business of the world has taken place. It has happened so quickly that no one can entirely explain it. It has been like an awakening of the human race to a universal spirit of competition. The entire world set to work. All the peoples of the earth demonstrated their energy, and each country, even the smallest, stepped forward into the public eye.

Yet though all countries show epochal changes in their nineteenth-century histories, the United States has outdone itself. Still small and weak one hundred years ago, it is now the mightiest republic under the sun. It can demand respect from all the nations of the earth. Its commerce has spread throughout the world. The citizens of our country are—to speak with the poet—grown one with their higher purposes. The freedom that inspired them sparked their genius, their diligence, and their entrepreneurial spirit.

We owe our progress to no monarch; the American spirit brought all this about. It is customary to congratulate one another on New Year's Day, and it is fitting to extend these congratulations at the beginning of a new century to the entire world: long live "Uncle Sam," may he grow and thrive! May he continue to prepare the way for freedom and to demonstrate to the world the blessings of government by and for the people.

Racine Daily Journal, December 31, 1900

The Nineteenth century passes out and the scroll of time brings to view the Twentieth century. Its dawn discovers the world expectant, yet triumphant at the remarkable progress that has been made during the long years in every department of industry, science and commerce. In the realms of speculation, in those of chemistry, in geology and of astronomy, there does not seem much to be left for the future discoveries that can arouse a world. Our earth so small, yet so very large, yet has wonderful regions that for practical purposes are utterly unknown. Vast tracts of land left behind in the movements of mankind, are yet to be mapped, and this work is progressing year by year, and in a sort of way man is determining the full extent of the heritage given him by his Creator. . . .

In the past hundred years the world at large has prospered and developed and in all the list of countries, there is none that can compare with the glorious republic of the United States. One hundred years ago, a decade previous having set upon business for ourselves after a war for independence last[ing] seven years, our country had an area of 827,844 square miles with thirteen states. . . .

The great west was a blank on the map a hundred years ago and the English, the Spanish and French held vast stretches of country which is today under our flag. All west of the Mississippi was foreign territory and all of Florida was Spanish. In the far northwest the Columbia river remained to be located and not until 1803, through the wonderful expedition of Lewis and Clark, was [discovered] the riches of that are now Oregon and Washington and the mountain country—now the states of Dakota, Montana, Wyoming, Idaho. General Fremont later on added to our information stores of knowledge concerning the now great mining country, Utah and California. Spain yielded her possessions, then came France, then the 54:40 or fight gave us Washington and Oregon practically. Then came along the war with Mexico and gave us New Mexico, Utah and California, with a few years later the Gadsden purchase more of Mexican territory, Texas had come into the Union through her own prowess and added millions of additional square miles of territory and some thousands of brave men; Texas now a state of over 2,000,000 people and of wonderful resources.

What will the next hundred years bring forth? It is a mystery of the future in one way and in another no mystery, for with the astounding progress in the arts, sciences, agriculture and manufactures and with the constantly increasing population, it hardly requires a prophet to foretell what we will be ten decades hence.

We have been blessed as no other nation has and in our prosperity we do not forget the obligations we owe to the Creator of all who has so richly endowed us as a nation. Let the new year be one of peace, of prosperity and as the first of the new century marked by acts of wise statesmanship. Let us hope the cruel war in the Philippines may speedily terminate and all over our broad land extend the folds of the American flag waving over a happy and contented and peaceful people.

All hail the New Year!

"American Enterprise and Ingenuity"

American prosperity was built on a foundation of rising agricultural and industrial production. Wisconsin played an important role in this development, and according to the author of the following article, one of the heroes of nineteenth-century agricultural development was the better-bred bovine.

(Racine) Wisconsin Agriculturalist, January 3, 1901

THE TWENTIETH CENTURY COW

She is a very different creature from the cow which saw the dawn of the nineteenth century. Yes; even fifty years ago the cow of our fathers' yard had little in common with the fine specimen we call the queen of the stable today. We all know what she had in the way of ancestry. Hardly a cow in the country half a century ago could boast of a lineage worth preserving. Her care and general treatment comported well with her descent. She stood half the winter long out in the cold, shivering, hungry and a standing advertisement of the fact that her owner considered her simply an adjunct of his farm rather than his most valuable assistant.

But the cow of the new century! She opens her eyes upon a prospect most delightful to contemplate. She is recognized as furnishing the lucky man who possesses her a most desirable part of his income from year to year. The millions of dollars invested in her and her progeny in this country according to the latest census show that she represents a quantity upon the dairyman's cashbook by no means inconsiderable. Then, too, her surroundings are fairly palatial compared with those of her grandmother. It is now thought worth while to provide her with warm quarters, secure from the wintry blasts; to furnish her with the best of hay and corn and other feed; to keep her well supplied with pure and fresh water; to shield her even from the flies which might annoy her and detract from her peace of body; in short, to do everything possible to add to her comfort.

Her pedigree is carefully traced and hung in the parlor where all may point to it with pride. From calfhood to full maturity she is an object of the utmost consideration, and her untimely departure, in case such should be her fate, is the source of deepest lamentation.

What does the new century cow do to compensate for all this watchful solicitude? According to the statistical report for 1898, the latest before me, there are about 16,000,000 cows in this country, valued at $474,000,000. Not far from ten thousand creameries are in operation in which 300,000,000 pounds of butter are made each year, or one-fifth of the total output, the remaining 1,200,000,000 pounds represents the labor of private dairies. The value of every pound of butter made should be at least twenty cents, from which we may conclude that the worth of the butter alone which our cow gives us every year is about $3,000,000. Besides there is the cheese, the tallow, the hides and all the other products traceable to the cow.

What a beautifully magnificent creature she is! We do well to take pride in her. She repays all our efforts in her behalf ten fold every year. Do we sufficiently appreciate her consequence in our farm economy? Some do not. That is sure. They still consider her just as their grandfathers did, as an animal to be tolerated on the farm. It is time these men woke up to the fact that the cow is a creature of flesh of blood, with keen instincts and a sharp sense of justice. With what measure we mete to her, with that measure she returns. She is a business animal. She knows when she is fairly dealt with and responds accordingly.

It will pay us to cultivate more carefully the acquaintance of the new century cow.

The government, of course, played an important role in the development of American foreign and domestic trade. This article, from a Republican newspaper, gives much of the credit to the administration of President William McKinley.

(Friendship) Adams County Press, *December 30, 1899.*

Janesville Daily Gazette, January 2, 1901

It is gratifying to know that America enters the new century leading the procession of nations in the value of exports. The United
States has been forging rapidly ahead during the past four years,
distancing all rivals except the United Kingdom, and passing her

on the last quarter stretch. The nation is recognized today, not only as the great cereal producing nation, but as the great manufacturing nation of the world.

Two or three things have contributed to the wonderful conditions.

The first, American enterprise and ingenuity, both of which are without a parallel. Chicago capital is now building four ocean freighters that will cost $1,000,000. They will be loaded with machinery and manufactured goods, and sail from Chicago for the old world early in April. So far as heard from, no subsidy is expected.

The second is a wise administration that possessed the foresight and courage to adopt a protective tariff that enabled our industries, not only to get on their feet, but to walk out independently and meet the world's competition. It accomplished more than this, for the encouraged industries took on new life, until every wheel in every factory, everywhere throughout the broad land, was turning, while American labor, contented and happy, contributed to the busy hum. Prosperity within our borders followed as a natural result, and a steady stream of money flowed in. The individual prospered and the nation prospered, until four short years filled a bankrupt treasury with abundant wealth.

The wise administration did more than this. It settled for all time the question of national honor, so far as sound financial policy was concerned, and today American securities are in brisk demand in all the markets of the world.

If the Ship of State is wisely handled American enterprise will continue to reap the rewards to which it is entitled, and before the new century is fairly on its feet, many long strides will mark an era of rapid progress.

> Wisconsin editors and writers also noted that America's commercial growth and geographic expansion had been accompanied by a tremendous increase in the size of the federal government.

Superior Evening Telegram, January 4, 1901

The nineteenth century has been remarkable for the growth of public expenditures. Enormous debts have been created by the civilized nations of the world, the expenses of government have increased to a startling extent and the taxpayers bear burdens compared with which those of their forefathers were trivial. As Mr. Charles A. Conant points out in an article in the January *Atlantic Monthly*, "Burdens of taxation amounting in volume to many times the sum which drove our British ancestors to take arms against the Stuarts in the seventeenth century, or which impoverished France before the revolution, are now borne almost without a murmur by the people of every civilized state." . . .

The United States has also become extravagant as a nation. In 1842 the government needed only $25,205,761 for its expenses. Then came the civil war, when a colossal debt was piled up. The cost of the government upon a peace basis before the recent increase of the army was about $5 per head—more than three times greater, according to Mr. Conant, than it was 60 years ago, two and one-half times what it was before the civil war and 20 per cent greater than it was 14 years ago. The lowest per capita expenditure since the civil war was in 1886, under the administration of President Cleveland. In 1860 the cost of river and harbor improvement was $221,973. The net disbursements in 1898 for rivers and harbors were $20,785,109. The postal service is not self-sustaining, and every year the government has to meet the deficit. Last year it was $8,211,750. The lighthouse service cost over $3,000,000 in 1899. The scientific bureaus of the government are expensive. Pensions cost $140,000,000 a year, or nearly $2 per capita. The pension expenditure for 1900 Mr. Conant states, barring one year of the Mexican war, "is not much less that the cost of the federal government for all purposes down almost to 1860. If the expenses of the military and naval establishments last year were added to the expenditures for pensions the burden upon the American people for these objects was about $4.40 per head, or very close to the entire military and naval expenditure of the Empire of Napoleon when he was leading the Grand Army of 600,000 men to its death amidst the snows of Russia." If the cost of state and municipal expenditure were added to the expenditures of the national government the total would reach an extraordinary figure. The annual cost of the government of the city of New York since its consolidation with Brooklyn is nearly $90,000,000. It is estimated that the salaries paid to school teachers alone in the United States amounted to $123,809,412 in 1899. . . .

Mr. Conant says in conclusion:

"The history of the century in public finance, therefore, and especially the history of the present generation, illustrates the benefits which may come to the community from a well directed use of a part of its new wealth in the extension of state functions. The character of this extension need not be radically socialistic nor disturbing to the existing order, but may simply relieve the individual of many minor duties which could not be performed at all before, or were performed inadequately or at great individual expense. Just as the average man has ceased to try to be his own carpenter, physician, or lawyer in spite of a breath of culture which may include some knowledge of their duties, he has ceased to undertake the many functions relating to public health, introduction, and protection, which were formerly performed by the individual, because he could not afford to contribute from slender surplus above the cost of maintenance to have them performed by others. The increase in public expenditures, great as it has been, has by no means kept pace with the increase of social wealth above the subsistence point, but has taken a fraction of these great resources and ought to apply it to those improvements in social condition which can be best provided through state action. Modern social development, opening new means of comfort and luxury on every hand to the mass of men, would be strangely one sided, if it left the functions of the state shut within the parsimonious limits of a century ago, or even a generation ago."

> In this piece, one editor suggested that as the government had grown, so had the pernicious influence of money on elections. This suspicion was not his alone; a week later the *Chippewa Falls Weekly* reprinted this editorial.

Mondovi Herald, December 21, 1900

One hundred years ago when the capital was located at Washington the financial problem attending the location, which involved the expenditure of half a million of dollars, was a serious one for the government to solve. Now it takes that much to buy a seat in the senate from Montana and she is not one of the greatest among the sisterhood of states, and many there are who can pay the price. Verily, times have changed.

"Who Would Have Believed It?"

> No subject captured the attention of Wisconsin's writers and editors more than the scientific and technical wonders of the nineteenth century. The following articles convey a sense of amazement at the tremendous changes resulting from technological progress.

(Union Congregational Church, Green Bay) Unionist, December, 1900

Prof. A. E. Dolbear, of Tufts College, in an article in the *Congregationalist,* on The Century of Science, puts in the following striking way, the progress of the last hundred years:

We received the horse and ox; we bequeath the locomotive, the automobile and the bicycle.

We received the goose quill; we bequeath the fountain pen and typewriter.

We received the scythe; we bequeath the mowing machine.

We received the sickle; we bequeath the harvester.

We received the sewing and knitting needle; we bequeath the sewing and knitting machine.

We received the hand printing press; we bequeath the cylinder press.

We received the typesetter; we bequeath the linotype.

We received the sledge; we bequeath the steam drill and hammer.

We received the flintlock musket; we bequeath automatic Maxims.

We received the sail ship, six weeks to Europe; we bequeath the steamship *Majestic,* six days to Europe.

We received gunpowder; we bequeath nitroglycerin.

We received the hand loom; we bequeath the cotton gin and woolen mill.

We received the leather fire bucket; we bequeath the steam fire engine.

We received the wood and stone structures; we bequeath twenty-storied steel structures on which the sky may rest.

We received the staircase; we bequeath the elevator.

We received Johnson's Dictionary with 20,000 words; we bequeath the Standard Dictionary with 240,000 words.

We received 22,000,000 speaking the English language; we bequeath 116,000,000.

We received the painter's brush and easel; we bequeath lithography and photography.

We received the lodestone; we bequeath the electro-magnet.

We received the glass electric machine; we bequeath the dynamo.

We received the tallow dip; we bequeath the arclight and the Standard Oil Company.

We received the four-inch achromatic telescope; we bequeath the four-foot telescope.

We received two dozen members of the solar system; we bequeath 500.

We received a million stars; we bequeath 100,000,000.

We received the tinder box; we bequeath the friction match.

We received ordinary light; we bequeath Roentgen rays.

We received the beacon signal fires; we bequeath the telegraph, the telephone and wireless telegraphy.

We received the weather unannounced; we bequeath the weather bureau.

We received less than twenty known elements; we bequeath eighty.

We received the products of distant countries as rarities; we bequeath them as bountiful as home productions.

We received history as events remembered and recorded; we bequeath the kinetoscope.

The lure of twentieth-century modernity was even used to market carriages and harnesses. Milwaukee Sentinel, *January 1, 1901.*

We received the past as silent; we bequeath the phonograph, and the voices of the dead may again be heard.

We received pain as an allotment to man; we bequeath ether, chloroform and cocaine.

We received gangrene; we bequeath antiseptic surgery.

We received the old oaken bucket; we bequeath the driven well and the water tower.

We received decomposition helplessly; we bequeath cold storage.

We received foods for immediate consumption; we bequeath the canning industry.

We received butter solely from milk; we bequeath oleomargarine.

We received the pontoon; we bequeath the Brooklyn bridge.

We received the hedgerow and the rail fence; we bequeath the barbed wire fence.

We received cement steel; we bequeath Bessemer steel.

We received unlimited dependence upon muscles; we bequeath automatic mechanism.

(Wisconsin School for the Deaf, Delavan) Wisconsin Times, January 17, 1901

If anyone in 1800 had predicted the wonderful things that have taken place during the century, he would have been pronounced as a fit subject for an asylum. Anyone predicting that the day would come when you could speak to friends hundreds or thousands of miles away and receive an instant answer as we do now by telegraph or telephone, would have been classed with the rattle headed. That we would visit Europe in less than one week, or travel over the land at the rate of one hundred miles an hour. That we could light up the body and see through it as by X rays. That boats could travel for hours under water out of sight. That your picture true to life could be produced in a second. That a sewing machine could be made that would do more and better work than many pairs of hands. That steam and electricity would be the powers that would run the machinery doing the world's work. That surgery—cutting a man nearly to pieces—could be performed without pain. That hundreds of thousands of copies of the largest newspapers filled with pictures, could be printed in a few hours. That air could be condensed into a liquid. That watches of great accuracy and cheapness could be produced by machinery. That the trees of the forest would furnish the material upon which to write and print. That bicycles and automobiles would rush through the streets of cities and over country roads. That grain of the country would all be sown, harvested and threshed by machinery. Had anyone predicted the foregoing and scores of other things that have actually taken place, no jury of his peers would have hesitated to pronounce him of unsound mind. The coming century will outstrip the past.

> Most Wisconsin editors and writers looked at nineteenth-century technical advances in an exclusively positive light. The author of this piece, for example, believed that the world was constantly improving and that those who disagreed had been misled because of the easy transmission of distant news.

Appleton Evening Crescent, December 31, 1900

The gates of the nineteenth century are about to close on the great inventive century of the world's history. Whether on land or sea the progress of the world has been wonderful. The utilization of steam and electricity has been marvelous, and in every trade and pursuit the improvements have been wonderful. "The old podanger days" can never return because there are no barbarian hosts to destroy the machinery of the present. From the flint-lock musket of the war of 1812 to the Krag-Jorgensen of 1900, or the old wooden frigates of 1860 to the battleship of 1900, and from the commercial wooden steamer of 1860 to the iron and steel passenger palace of 1900, how wonderful the stride. And yet in factory, mill and printing office, the transformation has been equally wonderful, and when one goes out to visit the farm the reminder comes that here too the pace has become a gallop. Looking backward, one is proud to have lived in such an age, and to have witnessed most of these triumphs of genius. Say what men may, the world has been growing better during all this period. True, the telegraph brings daily accounts of all the crimes committed on the continent, and many really believe the contrary because formerly they did not hear of one crime where they now hear of fifty, but they forget that prior to the telegraph not one in a hundred was ever published beyond the state or county where committed. Greed and selfishness may have increased at commercial centers of population, but morality and practical religion pervades the country as education comes more general.

The *Crescent* congratulates its numerous readers on the world's progress. They have done their part in the work, and will now enter upon a century that may and probably will change the map of the world, but there will be no backward steps in the march of humanity toward a better life and further improvements on earth.

> Though most writers celebrated new technology uncritically, a few argued that new inventions sometimes led to undesirable social changes. The following piece is part of an address that Minneapolis librarian James Kendall Hosmer made at the 1901 State Historical Convention in Milwaukee. Here, he considers the complex changes wrought by two nineteenth-century inventions. This piece is taken from the *Proceedings of the State Historical Society of Wisconsin at its Forty-Ninth Annual Meeting Held December 12, 1901 and of the State Historical Convention Held at Milwaukee, October 11–12, 1901* (Madison: Democrat Printing Company, 1902).

Proceedings of the State Historical Convention, October 11–12, 1901

. . . Lacking a thread on which may be strung, in convenient order, the details of the development of the Mississippi Valley during the nineteenth century, nothing better can be done than to trace the consequences flowing from the introduction of two machines— the steam engine as applied to traffic and communication, and the cotton gin. . . .

At the close of the eighteenth century slavery appeared to be dying everywhere in America: as it failed, the conscience of the land asserted itself as to its evil in a way quite new. It was the general expectation that negro slavery would soon disappear. It has long been held that the cotton gin, invented in 1793, by suddenly lending new effectiveness to the work of negroes in the South, wrought a change, spiritual as well as material—the economic advantage lulling to sleep the awakening moral sense. As years passed and cotton became king, slavery grew to be considered as never before, the very apple of the patriot's eye. Meantime, at the North, no economic advantage intervening to favor the preservation of slavery, it followed the course of decay upon which it had entered, and died out; and as the century advanced, it came to be regarded, under the influence of earnest teachers, as the chief of human evils.

Sundered thus as the North and South became in their interests and moral conceptions, a conflict was inevitable . . .

Strange indeed was the development which sprang from the cotton gin; scarcely less momentous has been the influence of the steam engine as applied to traffic and communication. The locomotive has succeeded, and often superseded, the steamboat, with results that are modifying all the continents. The new West, which has come to pass in the old Louisiana of the Purchase, was before the war in a most incipient stage, and as it stands today may properly be called the child of the locomotive. While that extraordinary machine in the eastern half of the valley has been a powerful modifier, in the western half it has worked almost as a creator. It has made possible a reclaiming and populating more rapid than has ever before been seen when new lands were occupied. The unknown wilderness of Jefferson's day has become filled throughout with fully organized commonwealths, and is about, with the admission of Oklahoma, to become, so to speak, politically mature. Whether such a rapid exploitation of the national domain will be for the ultimate benefit of our country, or otherwise, may well be questioned. Our grandchildren may wish their forefathers had gone more slowly. . . .

"Some Like Their Doctors Mouldy, Like Their Cheese"
In addition to the mechanical inventions that garnered so much
attention from writers, the nineteenth century witnessed a revolution in
medicine, as Dr. Benjamin C. Brett pointed out in the following address
at Union Congregational Church in Green Bay.

(Union Congregational Church, Green Bay) Unionist, February, 1901

The progress of medicine may not inaptly be likened to the advance of a conquering army in an enemy's country. Now at some point along the line of battle, an advance is sounded and a position is rapidly gained as if by storm, far in advance of the main line, only to be abandoned after night-fall, by retreat to a more secure position. Then at some other point along the line an advance is made and the ground is here held until the main line advances upon it, thus rendering the new position secure. And so medical history is one of continual advance and retreat but nevertheless one of gradual acquisition and permanent possession.

One hundred years ago the art of the apothecary was still crude, and, except in the larger cities, every physician was his own pharmacist, carrying his stock of drugs with him, mixing and dispensing them, in not very small doses, at the patient's bedside. Now and then a doctor was seen whose constant atmosphere was suggestive of the mingled odors of rhubarb, assafoetida, and decay, as though he were in truth a lineal descendant of Rip Van Winkle, and, like his progenitor, had just wakened from a twenty years' sleep. As Dr. Oliver Wendell Holmes once wrote:—"Some like their doctors mouldy, like their cheese."

Fads were as common then in the profession as now and phlebotomy was the first remedy for three-fourths of the ills of mankind. The lancet, calomel, tartar emetic and Spanish fly—each the foremost remedy of its class—were the agents most called into use. To be sick was indeed a great calamity. No wonder that people used to frighten their children into obedience by a threat to call the doctor.

One of the greatest contributions to medicine, marking a new era in medical and surgical practice, was the discovery and successful use of anaesthesia. Sulphuric ether as an anaesthetic was first used by Dr. T. G. Morton of Boston in 1846, and chloroform by Dr. J. V. Simpson of Edinburgh one year later. On the battlefield, in the hospital, in the reduction of broken or dislocated bones—in fact in every situation where pain or muscular spasm or severe bodily suffering of any kind is present—the surgeon can never do his best without anaesthesia. Many a time have I been called to a child with a broken limb who had cried itself to sleep before my arrival. Slowly administering the chloroform till the little one had passed from nature's sleep into an artificial one, I have adjusted the broken bones, applied the splints and bandages, and left the house, the little sleeper undisturbed, and still in dreamland. Is not this a Christian Science worth practicing? . . .

> Rapid advances in medicine also produced claims of miracle cures that were advertised daily in newspapers throughout Wisconsin. Dr. King's New Discovery was one of many patent medicines that claimed to cure colds and other illnesses.

(Superior) Inland Ocean, January 6, 1900

For amazing discoveries, for stupendous inventions, the 19th century has never had an equal. An electrician and an engineer sat in the Keokuk Hotel in Hannibal, Mo., discussing the question what is its greatest product? The former said the telegraph, the latter the railroad, but Mr. J. E. Lilly, who is connected with the management of the hotel, said: "Gentlemen: the greatest product and most wonderful discovery of the 19th century is Dr. King's New Discovery for Consumption, Coughs and Colds. The reason is plain. A discovery by which many thousands of lives are saved every year is infinitely more important than that which promotes a man's convenience. I know what this grand remedy will do, for it saved my life. I was taken with typhoid fever, that left a severe case of Pneumonia, my lungs became hardened and I got so weak I couldn't even sit bolstered up in bed. No doctor or medicine gave me any relief. I expected to die of Consumption. Then I happened to see this marvelous medicine advertised, and bought a 50-cent bottle. It gave immediate relief. I continued to use it until I am now a well and strong man. Now, gentlemen, when you think that 100,000 consumptives die annually in this country, alone, and that many thousands of them might be saved by using Dr. King's New Discovery, you will see I am right in saying it's the greatest discovery of the century." This medicine is the grandest cure on earth for Consumption, Stubborn Coughs, Severe Colds, Bronchitis, Asthma, Pleurisy, La Grippe, Hemorrhage, Hay Fever, Pneumonia, Lung Fever, Croup, Whooping Cough, and all bronchial troubles. The first dose brings relief. Money will be returned if no benefit. Large bottles 50 cents and $1.00. A trial bottle free. At all druggists.

"There Are No Limits to Her Ambition"

By 1900 the situation for women in American society had changed dramatically, though not as much as women's rights advocates desired. In the first of the two following articles, syndicated author Gertrude Thayer expresses feminists' pride in women's progress and their eagerness to take the struggle further. In the second piece, Katherine King gives a "New Century Talk to Milwaukee Girls," defending turn-of-the-century young women from critics who found them frivolous and strong-minded.

Janesville Daily Gazette, January 4, 1901

The girl of 1801. What a vision that calls up before us! A shrinking, timid creature with narrow shoulders and lily complexion, a girl who was sharply reproved if she held decided opinions of her own, a woman who was expected to shine as an ornament in her husband's drawing room, but when weighty matters were brought up for discussion was required to stay meekly in the background and hold her peace. True, there were some daring spirits who occasionally broke all bounds and spoke their minds, but we know from Napoleon's attitude toward Mme. de Stael how such women were treated.

Can you imagine a modern girl bursting into a roomful of these ultra genteel ladies? To make things as bad as possible, fancy her in a golf costume with her hair blown about by the wind and her cheeks tanned and perhaps a little dusty. How the mouths of our ancestors would have pursed up in disapproval at the sight of her mannish vest and her high collar and ascot tie. And if, thrusting her hands in her pockets and crossing her knees in a characteristic boyish attitude, she had regaled them with up to date conversation, don't you suppose that before she had been in the room five minutes the entire assemblage would have had a fit of the vapors, or fainted, or indulged in some other nervous performance fashionable at the time?

And would you blame them when you consider what the status of woman was in their time? Let me quote from the records of the National American Woman's association:

"In 1800 married women were not permitted in any country to control their property nor to will it away at death. To all intents and purposes they did not own it. The legal existence of the wife was so merged in that of her husband that she was said to be 'dead in law.' Not only did he control her property, collect and use her wages, select the food and clothing for herself and children, but to a very large extent he controlled her 'freedom of thought, speech and action.' If she disagreed with him or in any way offended him he possessed the legal right, upheld by public opinion, to punish her, the courts only interfering when the chastisement exceeded the popular idea in severity. At this time it was held by courts in England and the United States that a man in whipping his wife should be restricted to a stick no thicker than his thumb.

"All possessions passed into the hands of the husband at marriage. If a married woman worked for wages, she could not legally collect them, as they belonged to her husband. She could not make a will, sue or be sued. Few occupations were open to women.

"No college in the world admitted women. Men had so long done the thinking for the average woman it was universally believed that no woman was capable of mastering the higher

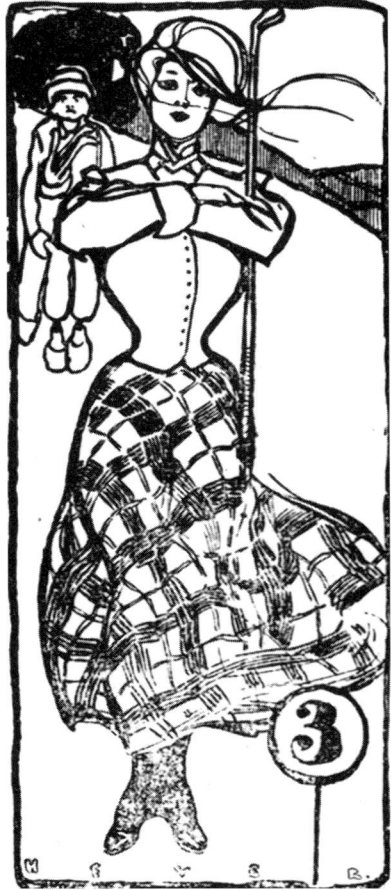

The American woman, from the "shrinking, timid creature" of 1801 to 1901's athletic and confident "modern girl." Janesville Daily Gazette, *January 4, 1901.*

branches of learning. The few women of genius who had appeared from time to time were pronounced the 'exception which proves the rule.' The convents and boarding schools wherein girls of wealth were educated taught nothing but the rudiments, while the girls of the poor received no education at all. Public schools were in many places closed to girls, and when admitted they were dissuaded from attempting the study of all branches except reading, writing and elementary arithmetic. Women were forbidden to speak or pray in the churches and, in many of them, even to sing in the choir.

"In 1803 a man sold his wife as a cow in the Sheffield market, England, for a guinea. Newspapers commented upon it as a common occurrence. The pulpits at this time gave frequent expositions of the necessary subordination of women, quoting from St. Ambrose as though inspired: 'Adam was beguiled by Eve, not Eve by Adam. It is just that woman should take as her ruler him whom she incited to sin, that he may not fall a second time through female levity.'

"It was upon such conditions that the curtain of the nineteenth century rose, the century which the prophetic voice of Victor Hugo proclaimed to be the 'century of woman.' "

We all know what she has gained. She works side by side with men, and her work is taken seriously. She receives the same education as her brother. She excels in nearly every branch of labor open to men. Marriage is not the only future open to her, but when she does marry it is no longer a slavery, but a partnership on equal terms. She refuses to be kept in ignorance of the world, and she faces it with clear eyes and keen judgment. She is healthy and athletic, as full of life and spirits as a boy, and above all there are no limits to her ambition. . . .

Milwaukee Journal, December 29, 1900

Such a line of ancestresses as she has—this twentieth century girl!

When she begins life next Tuesday morning she must take just a look back at them. Nineteen, in a great gallery it has taken 1,900 years to build; and whose nineteen pictures have been more cunningly painted than anything Sir Joshua ever did.

What are they like—these nineteen women who will act as godmothers to the twentieth century girl? I don't know whether in your heart you believe them all to have been greatly the inferiors of girls of today as you know them. I don't know whether you look down on the twentieth century girl and think she is pretty sure to go backward. But I know what I think about her—this new, new woman who is to work for her own position side by side with the nineteen who have gone before.

The woman of the first century. That one does not seem to you a real woman, does she? When you see her pictured in white garments with a light about her head; when you see her on the journey into Egypt by night; and seated in the manger with the wise men, can you imagine her the first in the line that came after, with its gay little figures, decked out in powder and plumes and patches? Least of all, can you imagine her having anything at all in common with the tailor-made looking little person who stands at the end of the line, and is just taking her reluctant place as an ancestress, too?

From that first century woman to the girl of the end of the century seems a far cry; from her, who is before everyone the type of perfect womanhood, to the maid with the side-wise pompadour and the golf skirt and the shirtwaist and the many rings.

Now, I dare say that there is to you something a bit shocking at this succession. I dare say that, although you cannot quite tell why, you feel some way as if there is no justification in bringing those two, as types, side by side. And because you do feel that way, as I do too, I want to ask you two things:

First: If the comparison shocks you a little, as a nineteenth century girl, what have you as a nineteenth century girl, done to make it shocking?

And second: Can't you see that those two are not so far removed after all, as differences would indicate?

Because I can. And these are some of the reasons why:

When the nineteenth century girl is mentioned I suppose everybody forms an involuntary picture such as the one at which I just hinted: A picture all bicycles and golf and chic and independence. I wonder whether the nineteenth century girl has deserved that? I wonder whether she really does deserve to have fin de siècle a term of opprobrium as it some way is? After next Tuesday that word will be a dead letter, and peace to its ashes. The word was all right, but we said it wrong. The nineteenth century girl was always more than we gave her credit for.

We cartooned the nineteenth century girl. Our jokes and our stories and the half truths we told always exaggerated her. All her little foibles we magnified and called ourselves clever to do so. Just put away your idea of the nineteenth century girl for a little, and think of her as she really is, and see whether that succession from the first century is one so impossible after all.

What is the use of judging all women by the strictly fin de siècle girl—to resort to that term for once—whom we have pictured as

THE TWENTIETH-CENTURY GIRL

HER NINETEENTH-CENTURY SISTERS DRINK A TOAST TO HER FUTURE

Milwaukee Journal, *December 31, 1900.*

all chic and dash and no mind at all? Or why judge them by the women whom we have pictured as all mind—strong mind—and not enough chic and dash to make a presentable appearance? Why, the girls who are accounted up-to-date girls, and that's all; or the girls who are accounted club women, and that's all; or the girls who earn their living—none of these, as one class, has a right to be the type of the nineteenth century girl. Yet everyone who speaks lightly of her, has in mind some one of these classes in whom he has disbelief, and with whom therefore he classes all other possible women.

What of the nineteenth century girls who are true and good and sincere and square? What of the nineteenth century girls who believe in people, and do not account themselves weak to do so? What of the girls who work and contrive for others, who support themselves, who spend their time in work and fun and honest effort for others, altogether?

Haven't these girls, who are everywhere, the right to hear themselves called the typical nineteenth century girl at last?

And instead, we all look them over, and note a loud gown here, and a pert little face there, and a good bit of strong mindedness somewhere else, and we say straightway with uplifted eyebrows:

"This nineteenth century girl. What is she coming to?"

Well, I will tell you to what I think she is coming. I think she is coming to nothing but good. I think that if much that she does cannot be approved, more of it can. I think that she is all generosity and charity, and a good deal of the time she is all sincerity; because when she isn't sincere she doesn't always know it. I believe that in another hundred years, if we were all here to see, we should see a world of women that would do the world more credit than it deserves.

Why, see here. Suppose it had gone the other way. Suppose that instead of evolving what was beautiful in dress, and gracious in manner, and elegant in her house furnishing and table service—the nineteenth century woman had leaned toward linsey-woolsey and shingled hair and stone china? Suppose that her Indian and Norman and what not ancestry had cropped up in a desire to do nothing but menial service, and suppose she hadn't cared for pretty things, and up-to-date ways of doing things? Can you think how everything would have gone? Does any man, I wonder, believe that he would have had the same pleasure in going home to a wife who would have welcomed him in homespun and short hair, that there is in seeing her in a gown which he wonders at and is proud of, and who says things at which he laughs, and in which he delights—all the while he is telling her she is extravagant and frivolous too?

Some of the extravagance and some of the frivolity of the nineteenth century girl are about the most civilizing influences I know!

You think this doesn't sound much like a century sermon, perhaps? Well, I don't know. I don't know really why it doesn't. If you can come to believe a little more in somebody of whom you have made light, if you can come to see a good deal of good where you had looked for only a little, that is all a sermon can do.

I do want the nineteenth century girl to be better. I want her to be more sincere, and more business like, and more orderly, and more square. I want her to be broad-minded, but first I want her to know what being broad-minded is; I want her to appreciate her family and to be loyal to them; I want her to speak just as little evil of people as she can; I want her not to like to hurt people deliberately; not willingly to do any wrong at all. And I believe she will be like this.

I believe it, because I believe she is like this now, with all the little frivolities—civilizing frivolities I said. I believe that she is good.

And if you, for instance, are not—the thing to do is not to judge the rest. It is simply to realize that you are behind the times. You are too old-fashioned to belong to a new century!

So here's a toast to the nineteenth century girl, who, Tuesday morning, will welcome a new title with which she can do what she pleases.

The new title will be a heritage. Use it well. Believe that you are as good as I have said you are, if you are. But believe that everyone else is, too. And that will be new century enough without the calendar.

> Not all Wisconsin newspapers approved of changes in women's status. By publishing the following humorous poem, entitled "Fin de Siècle Grandmother," one editor expressed his ambivalence about how some women's lives were changing.

Dale Recorder, December 22, 1899

The grandma in her cap of snow,
Who by the hearthstone used to sit,
And in the firelight's cheerful glow
With flying fingers used to knit,
Is gone alack-a-day!

She used to make such gingerbread!
What seed cakes, too, she used to bake!
Fit for a king, the children said,
Was grandma's golden johnny-cake,
But she has passed away.

Quite different is grandma now,
Her office is a sinecure;
No wrinkles corrugate her brow;
Her hair is la pompadour;
She wears a demi-train.

She laughs at signs of flitting years;
No spectacles rest on her nose;
At things old-fashioned grandma sneers;
A lorgnette takes where'er she goes
Hung by a golden chain.

Coarse knitting work she does not love,
Though oft she spins upon her wheel;
Her ball dress fits her like a glove,
Her snowy neck does not conceal
The fashion of today.

Of cook-book rules she has no need,
On mental culture is she bent,
And Robert's Rules does grandma read,
She of a club is President;
And she has come to stay.

"Our Progress Has Been Great"

At the end of the nineteenth century, Milwaukee's African-American
population was still quite small, amounting to only 862 of the city's
285,315 inhabitants. The community was, however, highly self-aware and
had its own press, churches, and other institutions. In this editorial,
Milwaukee's black newspaper reflects on African Americans' important
advances during the past century.

(Milwaukee) Wisconsin Weekly Advocate, December 27, 1900

At the close of the century it is appropriate that we look back and
review the history of our race in this country during that period.
At the beginning of the century now closing, as is well known to
all of us, we were in a condition of pupilage and bondage. Some

few were the toys and pastimes of massa or missus, while the great majority were subject to a taskmaster as hard or even harder than him of ancient Egypt.

As time crept on to the middle of the century public sentiment began to be awakened to the fact that all human beings, white or black, were men and had their part to fill in God's great plan. This sentiment crystallized in the great abolition movement which culminated in the abolition decree of the immortal Lincoln during our Civil war.

The next step in our advancement was the fourteenth and fifteenth amendments to the Constitution of the United States, whereby we were received into the full citizenship of these same states, with all the rights and privileges connected therewith, and as being on an equal footing with people of all other climates or countries. That some states, exercising their state privileges have recently to some extent, nullified these amendments, is, in our opinion, so much the worse for those states.

Now, having been received into this full citizenship, what are the results we can show to the world as a justification of these several acts? We assert that, considering the long period during which our race was in slavery, it has progressed more than any other known to history during the same period of time. Statistics were given in this paper a few weeks ago, showing the value of property acquired during the last fifty years, the advance in education, in religious organizations, etc., fully proving this fact.

But, reaching the close of a century, we naturally reach the close of a year, and this year of 1900 has been one of very vital interest to the negro race in the United States. The action of the Legislatures of several Southern states is bound to have a far-reaching effect, as we have of late frequently pointed out. The discrimination in dealing out lynch law to a negro and not to a white man guilty of the same offense has also been frequently dealt with in these columns, and needs no further comment here. If our subscribers have done us the honor of following up the plan we have pursued during the past year in presenting to them all current news of interest to the race, they must have seen that it has been prolific in men and women of the race, who are rapidly forging ahead in almost every direction—in literature, music, politics, athletics: facts culled from the current news of the day.

But while our progress has been great—even marvelous, under the circumstances—the faults, for which we alone must now be held responsible, remain, and the greatest of these is in our opinion a lack of self-reliance—a remnant and heirloom of serfdom, and this must be shaken off. Perhaps the next greatest fault, and especially in this fair city of Milwaukee, is the want of cohesion, of comradism, and in their place a condition of jealousy and suspicion and envy of one's neighbor. Such things should not be. We must remember the words: "A house divided against itself cannot stand."

We wish at this time to render our thanks to all patrons and subscribers who have stood by us during the three years we have had the honor and pleasure of producing this paper. To them, as well as to all of our race in Milwaukee and elsewhere, we wish a happy and prosperous New Year.

"Our Splendid System of Public Education"
By the beginning of the twentieth century, education was available to many more Americans than it had been when the nineteenth century began. In the following piece, Green Bay school superintendent Frederick G. Kraege reviewed this expansion in educational opportunity.

(Union Congregational Church, Green Bay) Unionist, December, 1900

Of all the centuries in the world's history, the nineteenth century has on the whole recorded the greatest progress of the human race. Development so rapid, changes so startling, inventions so undreamed of, crowd each other in a whirl of confusing images when we try to picture this century and note its achievements. Indeed, in some departments of human activity greater advancement has been made during this century than in all of the preceding centuries combined. It may be safely asserted also that in no direction has greater progress been made than in education.

Rousseau first set the world to thinking of the child and its psychological development, but it was not until 1869 that the first scientific investigation of the child's intellectual life was made in Berlin. Since that time under the wise leadership of Dr. G. Stanley Hall and Prof. Earl Barnes of our own country, despite the ridicule heaped upon its enthusiasts by the skeptical, child study has become a science and a knowledge of the laws governing the evolution of the physical, intellectual and moral powers of the child, is regarded as an essential qualification of the teacher.

At the beginning of the century, any person who possessed a

limited amount of scholastic attainments was deemed competent
to assume the role of teacher; today it is regarded equally important that the person should understand the laws of the development of the child to be taught, and should be skilled in the methods of using the subjects of study to assist the unfoldment of his
powers. No definition of education now limits its meaning to
mind-storing, or to mind-storing with ability to reproduce at ex-
aminations what is in the mind.

The kindergarten became the first objective representation of
the great truth that children may be aided in their development
by supplying them with material to stimulate their creative activity
and by utilizing their self-activity and even their play to this end.
According to Froebel himself, the purpose of the kindergarten is
"to take oversight over children before they are ready for school
life; to exercise their senses; to strengthen their bodily powers; to
employ their awakening mind; and to make them thoughtfully
acquainted with the world of nature and of man."

No educational reform of the century has been received with
greater favor by the public than the introduction of physical and
manual training into the work of the schools. The feeling has
grown apace that the old education depended too much on
books; that it neglected the physical development of the child;
that it did not provide adequately for development of the creative
powers of the mind; that consequently it was one-sided and partial,
and that it tended to foster a distaste for common manual labor.
Manual training does not aim at the teaching of any one trade,
nor does it impart merely superficial acquaintance with many
trades; but it gives a thorough course on instruction, both theo-
retical and practical, in the principal operations of all trades, and
thus brings students a long way on towards the learning of many
trades.

Ever since the fourteenth century the demand for individual-
ism for representation in the schools has been made, but it was
not until this century that the significance of the individual as a
member of society has been justly recognized. With a view to supplying the needs of the individual, courses of study have been
multiplied and enriched, first in the universities and colleges, then
in the secondary schools, and lastly in the grades, until those who
have found it difficult to keep pace have become alarmed. The
elective system has been introduced into the colleges and secondary schools, despite the fact that many conservative educators still

WHi(X3)21189

Physical education was regarded as an important innovation of the nineteenth century. Girls playing basketball at the Hillside Home School near Spring Green, 1900.

question the wisdom of allowing students in these schools a limited amount of freedom in the choice of the studies that they pursue. The elective system, first introduced in our country at Harvard, in 1826, is regarded by President Eliot as one of the greatest educational reforms of the century.

The theory of evolution, which was at first bitterly antagonized because imperfectly understood, has permeated every movement of the century, educational and otherwise. It has shed a flood of light upon educational and social problems hitherto dark. Psychological investigations have established the fact that society is a vast psychic organism, that there is an evolution of society as well as of the individual and that social traditions and customs react upon individuals and are in turn modified by them. Instead of being opposed to religion, as was at first supposed, this theory, verified by scientific investigation, has been incorporated into the theology as well as into the educational and social theories of the day.

At the beginning of the century but very few colleges and universities were open to women, and separate secondary schools were maintained for girls. Today co-education is the general rule and the higher institutions of learning that do not open their doors to women are anomalies. Despite all predictions to the contrary, women have demonstrated their ability to rival their brothers and win a large proportion of educational honors. At the beginning of the century but few trades and none of the professions were open to women; at its close there are but few trades or professions in which they are not engaged. . . .

The century's progress in education has been truly marvelous. As the nineteenth century draws to a close, the educational outlook is full of promise. Standing on the threshold of the twentieth century, with such an unprecedented record of achievement we have reason to expect that the new century will give abundant fruitage to the work which has been done in the old.

> Colleges and universities also changed dramatically during the
> nineteenth century, as public institutions such as the University of
> Wisconsin made higher education far more accessible.

(Kenosha) Telegraph-Courier, January 17, 1901

The history of the closing years of the nineteenth century indicates that industrial and educational conditions in the beginning of the twentieth century will be just the reverse of the conditions at the beginning of the nineteenth. It is a remarkable fact that for the first two-thirds of the nineteenth century, or from its incipiency down to the close of the civil war, there was an actual decline in the number of students who graduated at the various colleges in proportion to the population. The demand for instruction in the liberal arts actually fell off in this country during that time, in consequence of the diversion into industrial pursuits of the most promising young men, to whom the reward of business was more attractive than the delights of learning. As a result, while the country was developing industrially and growing in wealth, the conservative influence of higher and liberal education was being lost.

The school and the college were deserted for the counting room, the highways of liberal learning for the thoroughfares of commerce.

The present great wealth of the United States is largely a result of this rush to commercial pursuits that marked the first sixty years of the old century. The movement was also productive of the antagonistic social conditions that are the heritage of the new century. An increase in wealth, with a differentiation in the two extremes of the scale, unprecedented in history, has been accompanied by an accumulation of disturbing conditions, which it will tax the wisdom and the patience of the present generation to deal with.

But the conditions that created the enormous wealth and the social questions which are perplexing the people of today, have turned upon themselves. There has been a reaction toward liberal education that presents, at the beginning of the present century, a state of affairs diametrically opposite that of one hundred years ago. What might be called a surfeit of wealth, created at the expense of the educational institutions and features of our society, is now being used in the service of education. The closing years of the nineteenth century witnessed the greatest endowments of educational institutions known to history. Cornell, Johns Hopkins, Chicago University and Leland Stanford, all the creatures of philanthropic bequests, have sprung into existence in a comparatively few years. Moreover, there has been a wide contribution to schools already founded, both state and denominational, such as the State University of California, which has been given a new lease of life by the magnificent gifts of Mrs. Hearst.

Thus, just as the momentous problems growing out of the strained social conditions are beginning to look most menacing, the identical conditions that promoted the questions build up educational institutions, in which men and women shall be educated to properly deal with them. Most important of all the educational institutions that the reactional wave of public sentiment is nursing to full strength is the State University. It is the climax of our splendid system of public instruction and the most representative and typical republican institution of learning. Like the government, it is "of the people, by the people and for the people." What it is capable of being is evidenced in Wisconsin, Michigan, Minnesota and California. What it is liable to degenerate to, unless given the most jealous care by the people of the state, is demonstrated in many of the twenty-three states outside of those mentioned, which support a state university. It must be guarded against the influence of political opinion or party interest, and even against the rivalry of great universities founded on the wealth of charitably inclined multi-millionaires, for no institution of learning is more directly and entirely the people's and so capable of absolute freedom from prejudice as the state institution.

It is a matter of just pride to the Badgerite that the university at Madison is in the van of the educational institutions of the land, and that it is a leading representative of that typically American class of schools, the state universities. But while Wisconsin has, by dint of years of endeavor, created a noble school of training, there are other schools of a similar nature, which, through constant changes in the legislature, and self-seeking party leaders, have not only had their development hindered but have been deliberately crippled. On the eve of what promises to be a great educational revival, it is well for the people of Wisconsin to prepare to protect their state university from these dangers and maintain the high standard it has achieved.

> In the nineteenth century, the deaf made remarkable progress in gaining access to education. The following article, which the newspaper of the Wisconsin School for the Deaf reprinted from an Iowa publication for the hearing impaired, lists the advances that made schooling available to the deaf in the nineteenth century. The piece also reflects the school's support for pioneering educator Thomas Hopkins Gallaudet's instructional method of combining sign language and oral speech.

(Wisconsin School for the Deaf, Delavan) Wisconsin Times, January 24, 1901

During the nineteenth century the education of the deaf was made possible in the following various ways:

The first practical system of instruction as introduced by Gallaudet and Clerc in America.

The manual alphabet.

The sign language.

The first college for the deaf in the world at Washington, D. C.

The industrial training in nearly all the schools.

The church work among the deaf.

The national and state associations of the deaf.

And literary, social, and mutual benefit organizations.

School and independent papers for the deaf.

Students at the State School for the Deaf, Delavan, about 1893.

All these factors have never failed to teach the deaf so success-fully that they have become able to conduct their business affairs themselves. What might have become of us deaf if Gallaudet had brought the pure oral method to America?

The educated deaf will always demand that nothing but proper and correct methods of instruction for the deaf be used. Con-demn any and all methods that really fail to bring about satisfac-tory results.

Some critics claimed that as educational access became more democratic, the quality of learning had deteriorated in the nineteenth century. Charles Francis Adams took on this question in an address at the dedication of the new Madison headquarters of the State Historical Society of Wisconsin on October 19, 1900. In his speech, Adams, head of the Massachusetts Historical Society and grandson of President John Quincy Adams, asked whether the readership for serious literature had fallen off in the past century.

Charles Francis Adams, The Sifted Grain and the Grain Sifters.
October 19, 1900

. . . There is a widespread impression among those more or less qualified to form an opinion that the general capacity for sustained reading and thinking has not increased or been strengthened with the passage of the years. On the contrary, the indications, it is currently supposed, are rather of emasculation. Everything must now be made easy and short. There is a constant demand felt, especially by our periodical press, for information on all sorts of subjects,—historical, philosophical, scientific,—but it must be set forth in what is known as a popular style, that is introduced into the reader in a species of sugared capsule, and without leaving any annoying taste on the intellectual palate. The average reader, it is said, wants to know something concerning all the topics of the day; but, while it is highly desirable he should be gratified in this laudable, though languid, craving, he must not be fatigued in the effort of acquisition, and he will not submit to be bored. It is then further argued that this was not the case formerly; that in what are commonly alluded to as "the good old times,"—always the times of the grandparents,—people had fewer books, and fewer people read; but those who did read, deterred neither by number of pages nor by dryness of treatment, were equal to the feat of reading. To-day, on the contrary, almost no one rises to more than a magazine article; a volume appalls.

This is an extremely interesting subject of inquiry, were the real facts only attainable. Unfortunately they are not. We are forced to deal with impressions; and impressions, always vague, are usually deceptive. At the same time, when glimpses of a more or less remote past do now and again reach us, they seem to indicate mental conditions calculated to excite our special wonder. We do know, for instance, that in the olden days,—before public libraries and periodicals, and the modern cheap press and the Sunday newspaper were devised,—when books were rarities, and reading a somewhat rare accomplishment,—the Bible, Shakespeare, *Paradise Lost,* the *Pilgrim's Progress* and *Robinson Crusoe,* the *Spectator* and *Tatler, Barrows' Sermons* and *Hume's History of England* were the standard household and family literature; and the Bible was read and reread until its slightest allusions passed into familiar speech. . . . The question suggests itself, were there giants in those days?—or did the reader ask for bread, and did they gave him a stone? . . .

It would be difficult to mark more strikingly the development of a century, than by thus presenting *Hume's History* and Rollin as typical of what was deemed light and popular reading at one end of it, and the Sunday newspaper at the other. As I have already intimated, they were either giants in those days, or husks supplied milk for babes. Recurring, however, to present conditions, the popular demand for historical literature is undoubtedly vastly larger that it was a century ago; nor is it by any means so clear as is usually assumed that the solid reading and thinking power of the community has at all deteriorated. That yet remains to be proved. A century ago, it is to be borne in mind, there were no public libraries at all, and the private collections of books were comparatively few and small. It is safe, probably, to assume that there are a hundred, or even a thousand, readers now to one then. . . . In 1796, also, there were not a tenth part of the institutions of advanced education in the country which now exist. The statistics of the publishing houses and the shelves of the bookselling establishments all point to the same conclusion. Of course, it does not follow that because a book is bought it is also read; but it is not unsafe to say that twenty copies of Gibbon's *Decline and Fall* are called for in the bookstores of to-day to one that was called for in 1800. . . .

"True Spirit of Religion"

Many Wisconsin newspapers noted that religion, like other endeavors, had changed over the past century. Of course, their evaluation of religious change varied with their beliefs. The author of the first piece, Thomas Edward Barr, supported religious experiments such as the 1893 World's Parliament of Religions in Chicago and began a nondenominational "People's Pulpit" at Milwaukee's Pabst Theater in 1900.

Milwaukee Sentinel, December 31, 1900

. . . The Nineteenth century folds away the most glorious story of human life in history. The rights of man have been defined and established as never before, until even China lifts slowly into national consciousness. Comforts have multiplied until we cannot think ourselves into the barren happiness of the Colonial days. The splendor of culture from brilliant genius is in the hands of the most humble, invention has transformed life, and commercialism, the development and satisfaction of the wants of man, proves itself the chief spur and agency of civilization.

The religious changes of the century are equally great. Religious truth has become the property of the general public. We can realize how fully the clergyman of a century ago was, in his domain, an intellectual autocrat. Now every novelist has his shy at the problem. Religion is a matter of present character and experience. Before we accept a man's profession of faith we ask, has he integrity in human relationships?—for we deny the divorce of religion and morality. Religion seeks a scientific basis and statement. Our beliefs were thought out in an age when there was no physical science. Hence, the development of science brought controversy. Now we demand that the essential harmony of religion and science be shown, and that the basis and nature and method of religious life be stated scientifically, just as is done in any branch of truth.

The whole fabric of teachings based on the idea of fear has broken down. The reaction to scepticism is only temporary. Men are coming to a sane view of God in the true faith of all the ages. The humanitarian side of religion is in the foreground. Hence, the religious sentiment of our day has a glad freeness which was not a century since, but which makes possible a fellowship of honest spirits, as was shown in the Parliament of Religions, and which is the secret of our developing sense of brotherhood. Only in method we are still laggard. The principles of management which have built up our great industries are followed by few religious orders, and they are the ones whose work grows apace.

The same wealth of knowledge and power and opportunity which in all other ways makes resplendent the opening of the Twentieth century brightens and hallows the future of our religious life. We are getting a closer definition of the function and province of religion. In olden days religion covered every detail of life from birth to burial. Many now say it should be wholly set aside, save to influence children and to give man hope when he leaps from his death bed into the dark. We say it must inform life with an influence affecting every detail.

The function of religion is to establish the mind and heart in the truth concerning the Unseen and our relationships to it; and to develop and establish the character and present relationships of manly emphasis on the worth and dignity of the spiritual nature of all men. Hence, the province of religion is not to teach medicine or sanitation, literary criticism, politics or sociology, but to show that men are linked in a subtle and vital brotherhood as all children of the living God; that all true progress is toward and in the realization of this; that the Unseen is the potency of all present life. We traverse all fields, to find and rejoice over and insist upon the true spirit of religion. . . .

Ripon Advance Press, December 28, 1899

A hundred years ago stern theology taught that lunacy was possession by the devil and that the unsound in mind should be punished on earth in order that they might escape damnation hereafter; it taught that epidemics resulted, not from the violation of nature's laws, but from the wrath of the Divine Being, manifested for sins frequently entirely unconnected with the causes of the frightful pestilence; it still countenanced belief in witchcraft, it opposed vaccination and other preventives of disease, it upheld slavery, and it persecuted those who dared to differ from any of its teachings. A hundred years ago a Christian thought it his religious duty to refuse all dealings with an atheist, and that opprobrious term was more often bestowed then than now; a Unitarian was an object of bitter dislike to an Episcopalian, a Baptist believed that a Quaker would not go to heaven, a strict Presbyterian refused to allow his daughter to wed one who was not a church member, and in England, Jews were denied legal privileges.

> During the nineteenth century, Catholics had grown from a small minority to one of the largest religious groups in America. Catholic influence was especially apparent in Wisconsin with its large Polish and German communities.

(Milwaukee) Catholic Citizen, December 29, 1900

There have been many wonderful things which have profoundly influenced the destinies of men, both for weal and for woe, that date their birth during some of the eventful years of this century; but great as they are, we cannot but consider the welfare of the Church of God as the greatest of all. In all ages, through her divine organization as well as through the gifts she bears unto men, she can easily lay claim to being the most potent factor in the social and intellectual evolution of man. She lifted man up from the condition of serfdom and endowed him with both civil and religious freedom; she elevated woman; she inspired the arts; she trained the barbarian and taught him the highest civic virtues; she created the modern civilization which we enjoy. In estimating the factors that have influenced the lives of men she must be given a place far ahead of all the others. As there is no passion so strong in the human heart as that of religion, she who is the external embodiment of it has moulded and modified the ways of men as no other power has done. In making a hasty survey of the last one hundred years it is from her point of view we must look, and through her eyes we must estimate the progress of the world.

She began the century with little hope of securing many triumphs during its course. She was down in the valley of the shadow of death. The wise men of the world seemed to see in her a hoary old institution, bearing with some dignity the laurels of the past, though feebly tottering to her ruin. Judged from worldly standards, there did not appear to be any elements of recuperation within her bosom; her strength was sapped in the wrinkles and emaciation of old age. The signs of the times were portentous. The spirit of religion had been drowned in the streams of blood of the Revolution in France. England and Germany, who had been nourished at the breasts of the Church, had gone out from under her roof-tree and had disowned her for the poisonous pastures of heresy. Russia and the East were in decadent schism. Austria, like a spoiled child, attempted to rule the household. Italy and Spain defended their old home, but it was with many insults to their feeble mother. Humanly speaking, there was but little hope that the Church would ever rise from her bed of prostration and defeat. But the ways of God are not the ways of men. "Why have the Gentiles raged and the people devised vain things?" "The kings of the earth stood up, and the princes met together against the Lord and against his Christ." "Let us break their bonds asunder, and let us cast away their yoke from us. He that dwelleth in heaven shall laugh at them; and the Lord shall deride them. Then shall he speak to them in his anger and trouble them in his rage. But I am appointed king by him over Sion, his holy mountain, preaching His commandments. The Lord had said to me: Thou art my son, this day have I begotten thee. Ask of me, and I will give thee the Gentiles for thy inheritance, and the uttermost parts of the earth for thy possession. Thou shalt rule them with a rod of iron, and shall break them in pieces like a potter's vessel."

The princes of the earth had raged against the Church and the people had devised vain things, and now, after every antagonist has exhausted the resources of his energies, she has the Gentiles for her inheritance and the uttermost bounds of the earth for her possession.

Many Wisconsin residents judged the century's changes in a religious light. The author of the following piece wondered whether the material advances of the past hundred years had been matched by moral progress, and how religion and morality might guide humanity in the century to come.

Green Bay Advocate, January 4, 1901

Another century has dawned. Of the centuries past no one has witnessed such wonderful development of the powers and capabilities of the human race as the period of one hundred years just completed.

As the beginning of a new year is by general consent recognized as a time for starting reforms, for "swearing off" and desisting from past evil practices, the beginning of a new century is a time for retrospection and survey of the past and a determination to recognize and correct its evils.

The prominent feature of the world's history of the past hundred years is the remarkable advance that has been made in methods of production, in the things that tend to material prosperity. Along this line the advance during the past century has been marvelous. This progress has been more and more rapid in recent times, the growth of ten years past having been almost as great as that of the first half of the century. It seems as if development in this direction had almost reached the limit.

The progress of the human race towards the ideal is not made by steady advancement along all the different lines in which its capabilities are being developed. Progress in one particular direction seems to be accompanied by a lack of progress or even retrogression in some other directions.

Thus while the advancement of the race during the past century in the development of those powers which add to its material prosperity has been the greatest ever known in the history of the world, there has not been a corresponding advance in other directions. The race has not made the advance morally that it has financially. The growth along the lines which tend to the comfort of the outer man is accompanied by a neglect of the inner life.

There are unmistakable signs that the present century will be marked by greater attention to the development of the spiritual side of man's nature. Within the past few years there has been a decided change in the current of religious thought. Slowly but surely the Christian churches are turning their attention to the remedying of unjust social conditions; are making the brother-hood of man a substantial, living reality instead of an abstract theory. Social reform is a prevailing topic of discussion. It seems to be the task of the Twentieth century to put into practice the ideals of life which have been vaguely discussed during the past few years.

During the Nineteenth century we have found out how to make the things that might enable us all to live in comfort. During the Twentieth century we must learn how to use these things so that all may be benefitted by them.

3

A New World of Technology

"The Unfolding Panorama of the New Century"

> While Wisconsin residents reflected on the glories of the past, they
> expected even greater advances in the coming century. Most notably,
> many believed that the twentieth century would be a time of
> unparalleled technological progress. Nationally known authors as well as
> small-town newspaper editors predicted new inventions and scientific
> advances that would improve the quality of life. While some offered
> detailed descriptions of developments in science and technology, others,
> such as the following two writers, offered more sweeping visions of the
> next hundred years.

Waupaca Post, December 28, 1900

The passing of the year 1900 marks the close of the nineteenth
century; it is the most important era, viewed as a cycle of time,
which any one now living will probably witness. With the New Year
and the New Century will come new and graver responsibilities,
for the older we grow the more we realize our position in the
world; the more fully do we appreciate the work which we, as good
citizens, are called upon to perform.

The twentieth century starts out with its people much better
equipped for life than did any of its predecessors. In the hundred
years just passed the advancement along the lines of education,
and through it in the sciences, liberal arts and mechanics, have
been most marvelous. When one stops to think that the application of steam as a motive power, and the use of electricity in a
thousand different ways, to speak of nothing else, have been the
products of the past hundred years, one commences to realize
how vast the improvement has been. The development has not
been confined to any particular science or line of work, it has been

general and universal. Much of the perfection of this development has occurred within the memory of the present generation; in fact, it may be stated that the inventive intellect seems to have reached its height during the last twenty-five years.

And yet, if one is justified in prophesying for the future by comparison with the past, what unknown achievements may be revealed within the hundred years to come? The outlook would be appalling were it not for the belief that education and enlightenment and civilization would keep up with the progress; in fact will be necessary to, and a part of it, and that the world will as quickly adjust itself to liquid air, to airships, communications with other planets, to the transmission of messages on thought waves, as we in the nineteenth century have accepted and used the steamship, the electric railroad, the telegraph and the telephone.

The century now drawing to a close has witnessed many great and sanguinary wars; let us hope that civilization will have so far advanced in another hundred years that universal peace will prevail, that nations will not send forth the flower of their manhood as targets for enemy's bullets, that lands and money may be obtained.

The old century closes with a prospect of combined capital bearing down upon the poor; let us hope that before the next one closes, the doctrine that all men are entitled to a chance to live, each with his share of the good things of the world, and that no one shall be rich, if it makes his neighbor poor—in other words, the doctrine of brotherly love, will be the universal law of the land.

(Superior) Leader-Clarion, January 1, 1901

The twentieth century is born.

What will we do with it? The mind of man cannot compass the possibilities of the forthcoming one hundred years. Why seek to prophesy? Who is there so bold as to declare that he can justly name the feat impossible of performance in the realms of science and natural law?

Who a hundred years ago, would have deemed possible the accomplishment of one fractional portion of the marvels that the man of science and the inventive genius of the nineteenth century have produced from their teeming brains? . . .

The material wealth and prosperity of the world, through the manifold and multiform products of the inventor's fertile brain, have been increased beyond computation the past one hundred

The baby new year in his steam-powered "New Century" sleigh knocks the old year on his back. (Superior) Evening Telegram, *December 31, 1900.*

years. The coming century will see the best of the old retained, while that which cannot stand the test of time and cannot meet comparison with the new must retreat before the ceaseless, endless, irresistible onrush of enterprise, energy and genius.

Whether the century that now steps over the portal of the ages and enters our lives shall see the dreams of the savants of all time realized, who shall say? In the light of the bygone century's deeds, is there any one so bold as to declare that the really impossible exists? That the border line between finite and infinite things has been drawn by the omnipotent hand, that its existence is known to by the unseen, but all seeing eye of Him who knoweth and doeth everything, we cannot deny. But who, of man's limited and narrow vision, can tell where lies that line between the mortal and the divine?

In the light of the electricity that plays about the living wires of the telephone and the telegraph—yes, and the phonograph and kinetoscope—who can safely predict that the wonders of the Arabian Nights shall have no place in real life? Who knows when the genii of the lamp and the ring shall rise to endow some thinker in his workshop, some savant in his laboratory, or some scholar in his library, with the power to pierce the almost infinite and give unto man that for which the human race has longed and for which it has struggled and toiled, thought and dreamed, for centuries?

Shall we say the twentieth century is to pass without the accomplishment of marvels we have either not conceived or, casually thinking of, have scornfully passed them by as the impossible? Who shall say we shall not see the so-called "impossible" made possible ere the twentieth century merges into the twenty-first— or our children and our children's children, since we cannot live until the dying embers of the twentieth century have flared up into their last brightness, ere they flicker out forever?

Who is so bold to declare that the alchemist, out of his hopes, prayers and dreams, shall not evolve the secret that has mystified and tormented the sages of all cycles? Shall the mystery of transmutation yet be solved? Shall the master of the athanor not bring us gleaming gold from the dullest dross?

Shall men not rival the swift-winged, sweet-throated lark, and fly through the air, in apparent defiance of the laws of gravity and all other natural laws? Shall we not, without wires and without any other material signs of communication, signal, and even whisper to, our friends and kinsfolk, thousands and thousands of miles away? Shall not the wireless telephone and wireless telegraph, now a hope, become a reality? Is the realized dream so much more startling than its archetype of today. When we speak to and signal the voyager on the smiling Pacific or typhoon-swept Indian ocean; when we thus greet the friend or brother at Manila, in Paris, on ancient Nineveh's site, in Alexandria or in Stamboul, will it be more wonderful to us than our present greetings would seem to Sir Walter Raleigh, to Roger Williams, or perhaps to George Washington if these noted dead should rise today?

Shall the twentieth century see us out-Verne Verne and indulge in annual jaunts to the great orb of light that sheds its luster over our world with the daily sinking to slumber of the more fiery orb that rules by day? Shall a "trip to the moon" forever be impossible?

Shall the twentieth century behold the savant in his strangely-scented laboratory, pungent with the perfumes of a thousand volatile drugs and essences, and shall it hear him cry in accents full of almost delirious joy: "Eureka!" as he discovers, after years of patient thought and research, experiment and test, the compound that insures death to the terrible germ of tuberculosis—the dream of the Ecculapius of every age?

Shall the searcher after deathless fame, by glorious deeds of daring, discover the long-sought "Open Sea," and the "bright particular star" of every bold explorer's constellation of hope—the North Pole?

Shall the twentieth century see all or part of these things? Shall we live to behold the extension of the field of the finite into what we have deemed the infinite realm—because of our narrowed scope of intellectual vision? Who can tell? Unroll, and gaze back over, the scroll of the twentieth century, and if tempted to sneer or scoff at any prediction, however, strange or weird it may seem, pause and reflect before you assert that the unfolding panorama of the new-born century shall have no more thrilling wonders to reveal to a generation, perhaps yet unborn.

German-language newspapers still had a substantial readership in Wisconsin, especially in Milwaukee. Nonetheless, even readers of the foreign-language press had easy access to materials that originally appeared in English. The *Milwaukee Herold und Seebote*, a German-language newspaper, printed a translation of an essay by John Elfrith Watkins, Jr., a well-known columnist and author of more than a hundred mystery and detective novels. The text below is taken from the original English-language version that appeared in the December 1900 issue of the *Ladies Home Journal*, although only the excerpts that were translated for the *Herold und Seebote* are printed here. Watkins speculated widely about the changes Americans faced in the twentieth century.

Milwaukee Herold und Seebote, January 1, 1901

These prophecies will seem strange, almost impossible. Yet they have come from the most learned and conservative minds in America. To the wisest and most careful men in our greatest institutions of science and learning I have gone, asking each in his turn to forecast for me what, in his opinion, will have been wrought in his own field of investigation before the dawn of 2001—a century from now. These opinions I have carefully transcribed.

There will probably be from 350,000,000 to 500,000,000 people in America and its possessions by the lapse of another century. Nicaragua will ask for admission to our Union after the completion of the great canal. Mexico will be next. Europe, seeking more territory to the south of us, will cause many of the South and Central American republics to be voted into the Union by their own people.

The American will be taller by from one to two inches. His increase of stature will result from better health, due to vast reforms in medicine, sanitation, food and athletics. He will live fifty years instead of thirty-five as at present—for he will reside in the suburbs. The city house will practically be no more. Building in blocks will be illegal. The trip from suburban home to office will require a few minutes only. A penny will pay the fare.

Hot or cold air will be turned on from spigots to regulate the temperature of a house as we now turn on hot or cold water from spigots to regulate the temperature of the bath. Central plants will supply this cool air and heat to city houses in the same way as now our gas or electricity is furnished. Rising early to build the furnace fire will be a task of the olden times. Homes will have no chimneys, because no smoke will be created within their walls.

Insect screens will be unnecessary. Mosquitoes, house-flies and roaches will have been practically exterminated. Boards of health will have destroyed all mosquito haunts and breeding-grounds, drained all stagnant pools, filled in all swamp-lands, and chemically treated all still-water streams. The extermination of the horse and its stable will reduce the house-fly.

Ready-cooked meals will be bought from establishments similar to our bakeries of to-day. They will purchase materials in tremendous wholesale quantities and sell the cooked foods at a price much lower than the cost of individual cooking. Food will be served hot or cold to private houses in pneumatic tubes or automobile wagons. The meal being over, the dishes used will be packed and returned to the cooking establishments where they will be washed. Such wholesale cookery will be done in electric laboratories rather than in kitchens. These laboratories will be equipped with electric stoves, and all sorts of electric devices, such as coffee-grinders, egg-beaters, stirrers, shakers, parers, meat-choppers, meat-saws, potato-mashers, lemon-squeezers, dish-washers, dish-dryers and the like. All such utensils will be washed in chemicals fatal to disease microbes. Having one's own cook and purchasing one's own food will be an extravagance.

Storekeepers who expose food to air breathed out by patrons or to the atmosphere of the busy streets will be arrested with those who sell stale or adulterated produce. Liquid-air refrigerators will keep great quantities of food fresh for long intervals.

Coal will not be used for heating or cooking. It will be scarce, but not entirely exhausted. The earth's hard coal will last until the year 2050 or 2100; its soft-coal mines until 2200 or 2300. Meanwhile both kinds of coal will have become more and more expensive. Man will have found electricity manufactured by water-power to be much cheaper. Every river or creek with any suitable fall will be equipped with water-motors, turning dynamos, making electricity. Along the seacoast will be numerous reservoirs continually filled by waves and tides washing in. Out of these the water will be constantly falling over revolving wheels. All of our restless waters, fresh and salt, will thus be harnessed to do the work which Niagara is doing to-day: making electricity for heat, light and fuel.

There will be no street cars in our large cities. All hurry traffic will be below or high above ground when brought within city limits. In most cities it will be confined to broad subways or tunnels, well lighted and well ventilated, or to high trestles with "moving-sidewalk" stairways leading to the top. These underground or overhead streets will teem with capacious automobile passenger coaches and freight wagons, with cushioned wheels. Subways or trestles will be reserved for express trains. Cities, therefore, will be free from all noises.

Photographs will be telegraphed from any distance. If there be a battle in China a hundred years hence snap-shots of its most striking events will be published in the newspapers an hour later. Even to-day photographs are being telegraphed over short distances. Photographs will reproduce all of Nature's colors.

Trains will run two miles a minute, normally; express trains one hundred and fifty miles an hour. To go from New York to San Francisco will take a day and a night by fast express. There will be cigar-shaped electric locomotives hauling long trains of cars. Cars will, like houses, be artificially cooled. Along the railroads there will be no smoke, no cinders, because coal will neither be carried nor burned. There will be no stops for water. Passengers will travel through hot or dusty country regions with windows down.

Automobiles will be cheaper than horses are to-day. Farmers will own automobile hay-wagons, automobile truck-wagons, plows, harrows and hay-rakes. A one-pound motor in one of these vehicles will do the work of a pair of horses or more. Children will ride in automobile sleighs in winter. Automobiles will have been substituted for every horse vehicle now known. There will be, as already exist to-day, automobile hearses, automobile police patrols, automobile ambulances, automobile street sweepers. The horse in harness will be as scarce, if, indeed, not even scarcer, then as the yoked ox is to-day. . . .

Fast electric ships, crossing the ocean at more than a mile a minute, will go from New York to Liverpool in two days. The bodies of these ships will be built above the waves. They will be supported upon runners, somewhat like those of the sleigh. These runners will be very buoyant. Upon their under sides will be apertures expelling jets of air. In this way a film of air will be kept between them and the water's surface. This film, together with the small surface of the runners, will reduce friction against the waves to the smallest possible degree. Propellers turned by electricity will screw themselves through both the water beneath and the air above. Ships with cabins artificially cooled will be entirely fireproof. In storm they will dive below the water and there await fair weather.

There will be Air-Ships, but they will not successfully compete with surface cars and water vessels for passenger or freight traffic. They will be maintained as deadly war-vessels by all military nations. Some will transport men and goods. Others will be used by scientists making observations at great heights above the earth.

Giant guns will shoot twenty-five miles or more, and will hurl anywhere within such a radius shells exploding and destroying whole cities. Such guns will be aimed by aid of compasses when used on land or sea, and telescopes when directed from great heights. Fleets of air-ships, hiding themselves with dense, smoky mists, thrown off by themselves as they move, will float over cities,

Would even Santa adopt a more modern mode of travel in the twentieth century? Menasha Evening Breeze, *December 1900, supplement 2.*

fortifications, camps or fleets. They will surprise foes below by hurling upon them deadly thunderbolts. These aerial war-ships will necessitate bomb-proof forts, protected by great steel plates over their tops as well as at their sides. Huge forts on wheels will dash across open spaces at the speed of express trains of to-day. They will make what are now known as cavalry charges. Great automobile plows will dig deep entrenchments as fast as soldiers can occupy them. Rifles will use silent cartridges. Submarine boats submerged for days will be capable of wiping a whole navy off the face of the deep. Balloons and flying machines will carry telescopes of one-hundred-mile vision with camera attachments, photographing an enemy within that radius. These photographs, as distinct and large as if taken from across the street, will be lowered to the commanding officer in charge of troops below.

There will be no wild animals except in menageries. Rats and mice will have been exterminated. The horse will have become practically extinct. A few of high breed will be kept by the rich for racing, hunting and exercise. The automobile will have driven out the horse. Cattle and sheep will have no horns. They will be unable to run faster than the fattened hog of to-day. A century ago the wild hog could outrun a horse. Food animals will be bred to expend practically all of their life energy in producing meat, milk, wool and other by-products. Horns, bones, muscles and lungs will have been neglected.

Man will see around the world. Persons and things of all kinds will be brought within the focus of cameras connected electrically with screens at opposite ends of circuits, thousands of miles at a span. American audiences in their theatres will view upon huge curtains before them the coronations of kings in Europe or the progress of battles in the Orient. The instrument bringing these distant scenes to the very doors of people will be connected with a giant telephone apparatus transmitting each incidental sound in its appropriate place. Thus the guns of a distant battle will be heard to boom when seen to blaze, and thus the lips of a remote actor or singer will be heard to utter words or music when seen to move.

Wireless telephone and telegraph circuits will span the world. A husband in the middle of the Atlantic will be able to converse with his wife sitting in her boudoir in Chicago. We will be able to telephone to China quite as readily as we now talk from New York to Brooklyn. By an automatic signal they will connect with any circuit in their locality without the intervention of a "hello girl."

Grand opera will be telephoned to private homes, and will sound as harmonious as though enjoyed from a theatrebox. Automatic instruments reproducing original airs exactly will bring the best music to the families of the untalented. Great musicians gathered in one inclosure in New York will, by manipulating electric keys, produce at he same time music from instruments arranged in theatres or halls in San Francisco or New Orleans, for instance. Thus will great bands and orchestras give long-distance concerts. In great cities there will be public opera-houses whose singers and musicians are paid from funds endowed by philanthropists and by the government. The piano will be capable of changing its tone from cheerful to sad. Many devices will add to the emotional effect of music.

A university education will be free to every man and woman. Several great national universities will have been established. Children will study a simple English grammar adapted to simplified English, and not copied after the Latin. Time will be saved by grouping like studies. Poor students will be given free board, free clothing and free books if ambitious and actually unable to meet their school and college expenses. Medical inspectors regularly visiting the public schools will furnish poor children free eye-glasses, free dentistry and free medical attention of every kind. The very poor will, when necessary, get free rides to and from school and free lunches between sessions. In vacation time poor children will be taken on trips to various parts of the world. Etiquette and housekeeping will be important studies in the public schools.

Pneumatic tubes, instead of store wagons, will deliver packages and bundles. These tubes will collect, deliver and transport mail over certain distances, perhaps for hundreds of miles. They will at first connect with the private houses of the wealthy; then with all homes. Great business establishments will extend them to stations, similar to our branch post-offices of to-day, whence fast automobile vehicles will distribute purchases from house to house.

Winter will be turned into summer and night into day by the farmer. In cold weather he will place heat-conducting electric wires under the soil of his garden and thus warm his growing plants. He will also grow large gardens under glass. At night his vegetables will be bathed in powerful electric light, serving, like sunlight, to hasten their growth. Electric currents applied to the soil will make valuable plants grow larger and faster, and will kill troublesome weeds. Rays of colored light will hasten the growth of many plants. Electricity applied to garden seeds will make them sprout and develop unusually early.

Fast-flying refrigerators on land and sea will bring delicious fruits from the tropics and southern temperate zone within a few days.

The farmers of South America, South Africa, Australia and the South Sea Islands, whose seasons are directly opposite to ours, will thus supply us in winter with fresh summer foods which cannot be grown here. Scientists will have discovered how to raise here many fruits now confined to much hotter or colder climates. Delicious oranges will be grown in the suburbs of Philadelphia. Cantaloupes and other summer fruits will be of such a hardy nature that they can be stored through the winter as potatoes are now.

Strawberries as large as apples will be eaten by our great-great-grandchildren for their Christmas dinners a hundred years hence. Raspberries and blackberries will be as large. One will suffice for the fruit course of each person. Strawberries and cranberries will be grown upon tall bushes. Cranberries, gooseberries and currants will be as large as oranges. One cantaloupe will supply an entire family. Melons, cherries, grapes, plums, apples, pears, peaches and all berries will be seedless. Figs will be cultivated over the entire United States.

Peas and beans will be as large as beets are to-day. Sugar cane will produce twice as much sugar as the sugar beet now does. Cane will once more be the chief source of our sugar supply. The milk-weed will have been developed into a rubber plant. Cheap native rubber will be harvested by machinery all over this country. Plants will be made proof against disease microbes just as readily as man is to-day against smallpox. The soil will be kept enriched by plants which take their nutrition from the air and give fertility to the earth.

Roses will be as large as cabbage heads. Violets will grow to the size of orchids. A pansy will be as large in diameter as a sunflower. A century ago the pansy measured but half an inch across its face. There will be black, blue and green roses. It will be possible to grow any flower in any color and to transfer the perfume of a scented flower to another which is odorless. Then may the pansy be given the perfume of the violet.

Few drugs will be swallowed or taken into the stomach unless needed for the direct treatment of that organ itself. Drugs needed by the lungs, for instance, will be applied directly to those organs through the skin and flesh. They will be carried with the electric current applied without pain to the outside skin of the body. Microscopes will lay bare the vital organs, through the living flesh, of men and animals. The living body will to all medical purposes be transparent. Not only will it be possible for a physician to actually see a living, throbbing heart inside the chest, but he will be able to magnify and photograph any part of it. This work will be done with rays of invisible light.

"The Century of Invention and Discovery"

The new world envisioned in the article above was built on the belief that scientists would continue to discover more about the planet and the human body and make greater use of new technology. The first of the two following articles was reprinted from the *London Mail* and suggests the faith some individuals had in the capacity of technology to transform the earth itself. The second item shows how even paid advertising used interest in scientific advancement to promote products.

(Milwaukee) Union Signal, January 6, 1900

Few persons realize how completely of late years the surface aspect of this wizened old globe of ours has been altered and improved. The world of today, in fact, differs from the world of our ancestors, much as a society lady, in all the glory of fold and frill and furbelow, differs from her savage sister running wild in pestilential woods. As art has transformed the one, so it has the other. Only the "Mme. Rachael" who has made the earth, if not exactly "beautiful forever," at least a pleasant and healthful place wherein to dwell, is no charlatan with a dray-load of cosmetics and a glib tongue, but a civil engineer, owning nothing more harmful than a few mysterious-looking instruments and a measuring tape. And the marvel of it all is this—that what has been done is but an infinitesimal fraction of that which may, and doubtless will, be done. Who can doubt, for instance, that the great Sahara desert—that mole upon the world's face—will one day be but a memory? It was an inland sea once. It would not be a very difficult matter to convert it into one again. A canal sixty miles long, connecting with the Atlantic the vast depression which runs close up to the coast nearly midway between the twentieth and thirtieth parallels of latitude, would do the business beautifully. The water would not, of course, cover the entire surface of the desert. Here and there are portions lying above sea level. These would become the islands of the new Sahara ocean. What would be the results that would ensue upon this stupendous transformation? Some would be good, and some bad. Among the latter may be mentioned the probable destruction of the vineyards of southern Europe, which depend for their existence upon the warm, dry winds from the great African desert. As some compensation for this, however, the mercantile marines of the nations affected would be enabled to gain immediate and easy access to vast regions now given over to barbarism, and a series of more or less flourishing seaport towns would spring up along the southern borders of Morocco and Algeria, where the western watershed of the Nile sinks into the desert, and on the northern frontier of the Congo Free state. In a similar manner the greater portion of the central Australian desert, covering an area of fully 1,000,000 square miles, might be flooded. The island continent would then be converted into a gigantic oval dish, of which the depressed central portion would be covered with water, and only the "rim" inhabited.

DePere News, January 2, 1901

We now stand at the threshold of the twentieth century, and the nineteenth is a thing of the past. It will, however, be known as the century of invention and discovery, and among some of the greatest of these, we can truthfully mention Hostetter's Stomach Bitters, the celebrated remedy for all ailments arising from a weak or disordered stomach, such as dyspepsia, indigestion, flatulency, constipation and biliousness.

> The following article was part of a larger series of articles printed in the *Milwaukee Sentinel.* The newspaper's editors asked prominent Wisconsin residents to predict what changes the twentieth century would bring to their fields of expertise. Dr. Uranus O. B. Wingate, secretary of the Wisconsin State Board of Health, speculated on medical advances. Like many health experts of the time, Wingate argued that health and sanitation problems could be eliminated by preventing the reproduction of "degenerate individuals," which included criminals and the developmentally disabled. Although this belief in "eugenics" was popular at the turn of the century, it was discredited by the horrors of the Holocaust.

Milwaukee Sentinel, December 30, 1900

The advances that will be made in any of the learned professions during the next hundred years will be no less startling than those made during the past century, probably no more so, and the medical profession will furnish no exception.

Science is of a slow and exacting growth. She makes no uncertain strides into a dark future. Her devotees will continue to search for her hidden treasures in the future as in the past. There is no short road to her attainments. Those who bow at her shrine must walk in the rugged paths of patience, earnest endeavor, perseverance, honesty, and unselfishness. The medical progress of the future must be based on science. Without such foundation it would be only empiricism. The present fads and delusions concerning the healing art will pass away and others will take their places, but science will continue to advance and put to shame everything void of the living truth.

The medical student of the future will be selected with more care than now obtains. He will be required to possess a love for the truth and his chosen calling as well as to have a sufficient preliminary mental training. The mentally deformed and degenerate will knock in vain for admission into the learned professions. The enlightened public sentiment will recognize the scientific attainments of the medical profession and learn to value such knowledge, and while love for the mysterious will continue, human credulity will grow less and less as the profession becomes advanced in scientific achievements.

Sanitary science and its administration will become more exact and cease to be a work of charity. An enlightened human intelligence will dictate the justice of paying for value received. As the service of the lawyer which succeeds in settling his client's case without the expense and annoyance of litigation will be valued, so will the service of the physician, who saves his patient from an attack of illness, attend with loss of time, money, and perhaps life, be duly appreciated and willingly paid for; such a course will be true financial economy and the sum total of human happiness will be the result.

The springs of human life will receive greater attention, and the rearing of children will have the benefit of the advice of the truly scientific physician. Steps will be taken to prohibit the mating of diseased, deformed, and degenerate individuals, thus preventing the enormous influx of the defective classes now filling to overflow our almshouses, prisons and asylums—at least as much attention will be paid to this subject as is now paid to the raising of cattle and swine.

Upon this basis a new order of human beings will come into existence, and the physician will be relieved from continually meeting the vexed and intricate problem of inherited mental and physical defects.

Diseases feed upon degenerative processes, and degenerative processes are the products of disobedience of nature's laws.

A race will eventually spring up free from inherited defects, and by following the hygienic laws of nature, a people will exist practically immuned from infectious diseases, in other words, a race will exist possessing such powers of resistance, on account of their freedom from inherited defects and their improved hygienic living, that they will defy the invasion of infection.

A national organization of public health will be created by congress, properly equipped with all the means of study and original investigation, and with a well selected corps of experts, will devote its entire time to study and research, and co-operating with the various state health organizations, and they in turn with all the local boards of health in the various cities, villages and towns in their respective jurisdictions. This will constitute a great national public health system, both executive and educational, furnishing such information to the people that may see at a glance the progress or decay of the nation, and the causes which lead to either result, as well as the necessary remedies to be applied should they be required. Quarantine as it is now understood, which has been so destructive to commerce and public travel, will be abolished, and immunity and disinfection will take its place. The pollution of air, water and soil will be prohibited by law, and the construction of systems of water supply, sewage disposal and public buildings will be placed under the legal control of sanitary authorities. The relation of public health to commerce, manufactures, and all forms of industry will be considered of such vast importance that the best sanitarians will be engaged, and paid large salaries to look after their health interests, in fact such interests as will be considered equal, if not superior, to the legal relations of such concerns, from an economic standpoint. Human life will be held nearer to its full value, and there will be less neglect for the welfare of others. The medical officer in the army and navy will be required to possess a full knowledge of sanitary science, and sanitary attainments will be recognized to be equal in value to his surgical qualifications. Moreover, the sanitary orders issued by the medical officer in our military organizations will become the first law, and such sad and unpardonable results in the loss of life from disease, as have occurred in our past and more recent military expeditions, cease to exist.

The public spirit that builds a courthouse for $300,000 and an Isolation hospital for $300, that pays a judge a large salary for committing the insane to an asylum on the examination of a physician who bears the greatest of responsibilities and who is paid a mere pittance; that permits a public to drink water polluted by sewage, and children to be educated in unsanitary school buildings will pass away, and one will take its place which will interpret justice in a more reasonable manner.

The physician of the future by his education, experience, and training in human affairs will be considered among the best fitted to occupy positions in our halls of legislation and in public offices of executive function, and he will no longer remain on the outside and complain of the incapacity of others, and poor government, but will take an active part in public affairs and will be amply fitted to correct any evils that may exist. His advice will be considered of more value than his medicines, and he will occupy the position of a learned and honorable physician, citizen, and gentleman, and his children will rise up and call him blessed, and the world will be better for his existence.

> In the following article, the *Sentinel* asked prominent photographer Simon L. Stein to discuss the future of photography. Internationally known and a pioneer in color processing, Stein also served as president of the Photographic Association of America.

Milwaukee Sentinel, December 30, 1900

One hardly needs to be especially inspired to foresee that photography will, a hundred years hence, be one of the most important factors in nearly every department of human endeavor and practical achievement.

Its most important development will, unquestionably, be in the direction of color-photography, and the progress of that form of the art, even within the past few years, is sufficiently indicative of its certain and successful application to both commercial and artistic purposes that have been hitherto undreamed of, or only vaguely hoped for.

Already the surgeon or physician employs it to record, more certainly and faithfully than any written notes can do, the stages and varying conditions of a wound or disease, and the different

THE TWENTIETH CENTURY CALENDAR.

JANUARY

SUN	MON	TUE	WED	THU	FRI	SAT
		1	2	3	4	5
6	7	8	9	10	11	12
13	14	15	16	17	18	19
20	21	22	23	24	25	26
27	28	29	30	31		

IN THE NEW CENTURY NO ONE WILL WALK—ALL WILL HAVE WHEELS.

(*De Pere*) Brown County Democrat, *December 28, 1900.*

stages of an operation can be recorded as he proceeds so as to permit of the pictures being thrown up on a screen and explained to students in a manner that is not practicable while the actual operations is in progress. The botanist can show, by its means, the development of a plant from reed to bloom, as it actually appears in the field or the green house, and in the actual coloring of nature. The merchant can, in his office, see the color and texture of the goods he wishes to purchase as accurately rendered as if he was at the factory, but with far less trouble and in far less time.

So far as the direct registration of color is concerned that purpose is now actually accomplished, but we may naturally expect a further simplification of method as well as its application to moving pictures. To this end experiments affording excellent promise of success are already under way and I look for a successful realization of the plan in the near future.

Another direction in which great progress is inevitable is such a simplification of photographic methods as will permit of photography being turned to direct practical account in connection with every-day pursuits. The day will come when photography will be a matter of course with all and sundry—not for love of it, as a hobby, as it is with the amateur of to-day—but because it will be the easiest and simplest means of attaining certain practical results. When that day comes even the school girl diary will furnish an instance, for her diary will no longer be a written one—she will simply file away a pictorial record of each day's doings. . . .

The art of tele-photography will be greatly extended, especially in its application to war, as well as to engineering and other scientific purposes, the improvement being likely, in this direction, to lie in the construction of more suitable lenses and of some more effective means of trigger-action from a distance, to admit of timing the exposure when the camera has to be regulated from the earth—as when, for instance, the camera is sent up by a kite. The X-Ray will be even more intelligently applied to the study of solid bodies and we shall be able, by its means, to learn more of the structure of the earth, of the purpose and action of certain organs of the human body, etc., than any other method of research has yet enabled us to accomplish.

The wonders of the deep will be laid open to us, for we shall—as a legitimate conclusion to the lines of study that are now being prosecuted—be able to lower a suitably framed camera, with a light, and take pictures of "the deep sea and its marvels" that will teach us more than we could possibly learn by any other means.

Astronomical photography is now being pushed very earnestly. The "star gazers" have made, and are still making, some of the most remarkable discoveries their wonderful science has ever accomplished, and the photographic record of their discoveries enables them to register their data, and make them clear to the interested but unscientific public, in a way that assures us of knowing much, 100 years from now, of "the outer worlds" that we now cannot conceive of.

But it will be as a means of graphic instruction that photography will, during the next 100 years, make its greatest development and be of the greatest value. By its means, by enlargements upon a screen, every department of human knowledge will be thrown more widely open and more clearly demonstrated than is possible by any written or oral means. No description can, in the nature of things, convey "the mysteries of the stars and the wonders of the great deeps," the marvels of history and the splendor and ingenuity of man's attainment, so clearly as the actual present-ment of its image, in natural color, upon the screen. . . .

Streets of Grass

During the nineteenth century engineers harnessed steam power and wrought a transportation revolution with the invention of railroads, steamboats, and automobiles. The following articles, published in the *Kenosha Evening News*, predict that these inventions would continue to transform life in the years to come and that new forms of power would bring even more dramatic changes.

Kenosha Evening News, December 29, 1900

What will be the motive power of the twentieth century is one of the questions being asked at this time, when we are passing the century mark. So marvelous have been the developments in steam and electricity during the past 100 years that we may look for still more marvelous developments in the next hundred. No one can foretell to what extent human ingenuity may compel the forces of nature to do the work of man. Wave power and sun power are forces which may yet be utilized in turning the wheels of industry and supplying the propulsive energy of commerce.

The wave power inventor is at work and seems almost to have solved the problem of making the sea do the world's work.

Some day this great invention is likely to be perfected, and then it will be in order to see a transformation of our seashores into continuous machine shops. There is no doubt that power derived from such a source would be much cheaper than that derived from fuel. The fuel problem is not yet pressing, but if industries multiply in the coming century at the ratio that has prevailed during the closing century the generation of 100 years hence may sorely feel the pressure of this need. Increased use of cataract water power, such as at Niagara, has served somewhat to check the development of this crisis, and doubtless in the course of a few decades the water power will be utilized to the limit now dreamed of by enterprising promoters.

The sun power inventor is also at work, hoping to transform the sun's energy into a mundane motive force. In the light of past developments no one need marvel if the sun and the sea shall furnish the motive power of the twentieth century.

Kenosha Evening News, January 3, 1901

The *Electrical Review* thinks that the time will come when grass grown streets will be the sign of progress. And why not? When all freight traffic has been banished to underground railways and the automobile has displaced the horse for surface travel nearly the entire street between the pavements can be devoted to green turf. Cities of the twentieth and following centuries may be free from dust and the vile odors arising from animal traffic. The automobile mowing machine may be substituted for the sweeping machine, to the great improvement of health and increase of enjoyment of citizens.

Inventions

Americans displayed a vivid imagination with their predictions for inventions in the twentieth century. From "airy navies" of passenger zeppelins to electric matches to the wonders of liquid (compressed) air, authors speculated on a wide range of new products that would make life healthier and happier. Many Wisconsin newspaper editors consulted the work of Nikola Tesla, the Serbian-American inventor of alternating current and a rival of Thomas Edison, as a source of information on technological advances. The following syndicated article was written by journalist George L. Kilmer, who discusses Tesla, inventions, and even the Chinese Boxer Rebellion.

Dodgeville Chronicle, December 28, 1900

Were a prophet to foretell an advancement in manners, morals, learning and social and material progress for the next century equal to that of the last he would certainly be set down as a dreamer. Thinkers who are not pessimists believe that in many directions the limit, or about that, has been reached.

In mechanical inventions the nineteenth century achieved wonders which recall Aladdin and his lamp. Yet bold scientists declare that we may expect revelations of hidden energy in the sun and earth and air, which may be harnessed to do the work of mankind. Tesla believes in the possibility of a solar engine, he considers wireless telegraphy proved beyond a doubt, is working at a teleautomaton which will be simply a mentally endowed mechanism and declares that he has discovered electrical oscillations which will produce steady light without the aid of lamps, incandescent filaments or wires.

Tesla also predicts an industrial revolution in the dethronement of iron and the elevation of aluminum. He estimates the civilizing potency of aluminum as 100 times greater than that of iron and its bulk available for man 30 times greater. Liquid air, while a marvelous discovery, he holds can never be commercially profitable.

The sole aim of the scientist, Tesla insists, should be the increase of human energy and in that way the increase of human happiness. Material advancement is only a means to social advancement, and so after all the landmarks of progress are the monuments of social changes. The conditions of life for the masses upon this globe 100 years hence are of more consequence as a speculative topic even than the rare culture or superior development of a few or a class. What will be the conditions of life, and especially what the degree of immunity from grinding toil, from hunger and from disease, in the year 2001? It may be assumed that in the United States, if anywhere, the progress will be steady for another century. The country is comparatively new and its resources only partially developed. Should the population increase for the next 100 years in the same proportion as in the last 20 years it will then contain about 400,000,000 souls. In 1801 the population was about 5,000,000, which is but 1,000,000 more than the population of Greater New York and the Jersey suburbs today. New York should have a population at the end of the twentieth century of over 20,000,000 if its growth remains normal and proportionate to that of the whole country upon the above calculation.

At present New York attracts about one-eighteenth of the total population of the country and Chicago about one-half as many as New York. In another hundred years Chicago should have a population of about 13,000,000, Philadelphia 10,000,000, Boston, St. Louis and Baltimore each 3,000,000, Cincinnati, Buffalo, Cleveland, New Orleans and Pittsburgh 2,000,000 each and Detroit, Milwaukee and Minneapolis 1,500,000. In that era a population of 1,000,000 will be nothing extraordinary for a thriving inland city, and this conclusion is borne out by the history of densely populated countries in the old world.

The great industrial future which seems fixed by the hand of fate for this country will for generations at least tend to the growth of cities. Not alone that, but the attractions of city life will draw to them a mass of people still having commercial interests remote from the towns. The rapid means of communication will permit the landowner and the country manufacturer to dwell in the city the greater part of the year and still look after their business interests at a distance. And what marvels of cheapness and convenience those cities of the future will be. Municipal ownership of all enterprises which conduce to public convenience, the railways, boats, telegraph, heating and lighting plants, of libraries and perhaps of amusements, will reduce the cost of city life, which now appalls the economical visitor, to a merely nominal sum.

At present the tide of population sets toward the cities, and while this must change eventually a century is nothing in the life of a nation, and leaving out the probability of some great social upheaval forcing the people back to the soil there seems no reason why the commercial and industrial development of 1901 should not continue to the end of the century and not then have reached its limit.

The danger to health of massing millions of people in cities must be overcome by scientific appliances and discoveries. Cities of the old world have been depopulated by epidemics which would not be allowed to run their course today. The water of the future city will be pure, the temperature will be equalized, food will be scientifically preserved and prepared and men will more and more obey the common sense laws of health, avoiding extremes of exertion and stimulation.

Many propositions for the simplification of life which now seem chimerical may yet justify their champions. Condensed milk has

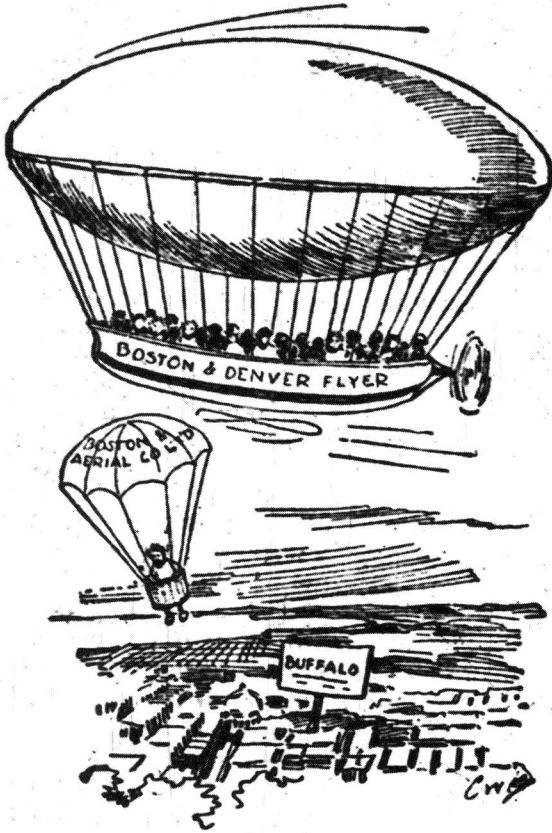

"The passenger for Buffalo can be 'put off' safely from a transcontinental 'flier' by means of a parachute. . . ." Dodgeville Chronicle, *December 28, 1900.*

stood the test of half a century of use, and other foods may be prepared in quantities by inexpensive labor and thus make it possible to live, if not on 15 cents a day, at least without the cost of maintaining a separate kitchen for every three or four persons. In that happy time there will perhaps be no necessity for reducing the hours of sleep to four in every 24, yet if the forms of entertainment multiply with other things everybody can keep awake 20 hours a day without suffering ennui.

The scientists tell us that even at the rapid rate projected for all forms of activity life and limb will be measurably secure. The perfected airship is one of the certainties of dreamers, but even

Tesla warns the nations who would be ready to cast about for means of attaining supremacy in the matter of "air power." If airy navies, then of course airy passenger lines. The passenger for Buffalo can be "put off" safely from a transcontinental "flier" by means of a parachute, and, although the artist won't believe it as yet, he need not wake up even, but have his berth transferred from the stateroom and slung under the ribs of the canopy. There he may finish his sleep as comfortably as did the nineteenth century tourist in a Wagner or Pullman at the terminal sheds.

Even war is to be robbed of its ghastliness, for, according to Tesla, machines will do the fighting of the future and sustain all the hard knocks, their human manipulators being out of range. Finally contests will come to be mere duels between automatons, and broken metal will figure in the casualty lists instead of broken bones.

Photography, a nineteenth century development, is on the cards for wonders greater than those yet achieved. Photography in colors is a certainty of the near future, and that wonder of the age, the typesetting machine, is doomed to fall down before the camera, which is to reproduce upon the printing plate text and pictures as set in order in the editor's sanctum without bringing in the aid of compositors or type.

The artist thinks that the Chinese imbroglio will not be settled until Uncle Sam can shout horse sense down a well curb into John Chinaman's ear. And that is no wilder flight of imagination than prophecies of nineteenth century marvels which have become commonplaces would have been on New Year's day, 1801.

> The writer of the following piece looked forward to more mundane inventions, such as the replacement of the match.

Racine Daily Journal, April 14, 1897

The electric match is the next important invention promised. Before very long the phosphorous tipped wooden splints now in use will be replaced by a handy little tool that may be carried in the pocket or hung up conveniently for striking a light when wanted. Twentieth century people doubtless will speak of the "hell sticks" of the present day as primitive and absurd, just as we are disposed to look with scorn upon the flint and steel of our forefathers. Already there is on the market a gaslighter which affords more than a suggestion of the electric match of the future, a twist of the handle generating sufficient electricity to accomplish the purpose; also there are several styles of cigar lighters which depend for their supply of electricity upon storage batteries. For some years past the gas jets in theaters and public buildings have been lighted by the electric spark. Indeed most persons have seen the curious experiment of lighting the gas with the finger after a shuffle across the carpet to generate the electricity needed.

The portable electric lighter is bound to come. Meanwhile inventors, as shown by the records of the patent office, exercise much ingenuity in trying to improve on the common everyday match. There are matches of bone and matches of pasteboard; also matches made of glass and matches of paper, while one enterprising genius proposes to manufacture matches out of a mixture of oyster shells and clinkers ground up. Not least interesting is a spherical match—a little ball of wood pulp, covered with phosphorous composition. In using it a holder is required, inasmuch as there is no stick, the ignited wood pulp burning slowly until wholly consumed. Thus there is no residue of stick and char to be disposed of, and matches of this kind have the further advantage that they are cheap and can be packed in very small compass, like pills.

> The following three pieces appeared in the *Milwaukee Sentinel* series of Wisconsin predictions on the twentieth century. Otto Martin Rau, who had electrified Milwaukee's street railway system, wrote the article below.

Milwaukee Sentinel, December 30, 1900

At the opening of the Twenty-first century, electricity will have a number of rivals which threaten to supersede it in many ways, similar to the manner that electricity is threatening its competitors today, the most promising of these being compressed or liquid air; but before these new forces have reached any importance in the commercial world, electricity will have been developed to a state of perfection and its possible applications will have solved the many apparently impossible problems brought forward by investigators and inventors of to-day, in a practical and commercial way.

We may expect to see the production of electricity so cheapened that gas will no longer be used for illumination and electric power and heat will be so universal that chimneys and smoke ordinances will worry us no more.

Electricity in railroading will supersede steam to such an extent that a locomotive will be a relic; our ocean steamers will have converted their coal bunkers into space for electric storage capacity; aerial navigation by means of stored electrical energy will be perfected; but while the continual improvement in generating and storing apparatus will cheapen the production of electricity, its application to the comforts and benefits of mankind is impossible to foreshadow.

> J. D. McLeod, a manager for the Wisconsin Telephone Company, wrote the following piece. In it, McLeod refers to Edward Bellamy, a noted author and journalist whose popular novel, *Looking Backward, 2000–1887,* offered a vision of a twentieth-century society based on utopian socialist principles.

Milwaukee Sentinel, December 30, 1900

Let me say anent the sphere of the telephone an hundred years hence, that Bellamy, in the full spirit of prophecy, failed to illuminate this question to any great extent, or to set a higher mark for its usefulness than we have reached to-day.

To an occasional tenderfoot, the telephone, doubtless, has its mysteries; and it may be natural to expect from its achievements in the past, new utilities and surprises for its future.

The fancies of Bellamy, however, have in practice become mere commonplaces to the telephone user, who, having every opportunity on tap, as it were, has long since availed of his predictions in the fuller enjoyment of the world's material and spiritual factors.

To the practical telephone man, the business is divested of all but its work-a-day aspect, and promises nothing more fanciful in its future than to lighten social conditions in just that degree we will be enabled to cheapen and popularize its use.

With the business essentially based on invention, improvements in the art will doubtless continue, and methods be devised to make for both, efficiency and lower prices.

Extensions, betterments, growth and improvement will therefore continue for some time.

As to trans-Atlantic connection, we are as yet offered little assurance of success. The best engineering minds are, of course, very active on that problem, and present limitations of transmitting through long cables may be overcome at any time. Practical work in overland lines is limited to about 1,500 miles, but in this connection it is interesting to note that President Glidden of this company, having the annihilation of mere distance in view, has offered $1,000,000 for devices that will accomplish for the telephone what the Repeater and the Relay have done for the telegraph. In this proposition we have the basis for one prediction at least not likely to go by default of inventive effort.

The chief promise for the future of the telephone is that its advantages may become common to the body of the people—that farming communities and the members of every hamlet may participate in its economies, and live in closer touch with their neighbors of the larger centers, and keep pace with the current affairs of the world.

To establish these uplifting conditions is the highest ideal.

> The author of the next article, Edwin Reynolds, also speculated on improved communications. Reynolds, an inventor who held forty-eight patents, was the driving force behind the Edward P. Allis Company, one of Milwaukee's largest and most innovative industrial manufacturers.

Milwaukee Sentinel, December 30, 1900

Can we not conceive it possible that at some future date we may be able to carry apparatus on our persons which will enable us to communicate with another person similarly equipped, anywhere on earth, without the intervention of wires, and after our experience with the telephone and the "X-Ray," is it not also conceivable that we may be able to see persons at long distances as well as to talk with them.

> Some authors and newspaper editors, like the author of the following piece, predicted that technological changes would affect a wider range of activities.

Oshkosh Daily Northwestern, January 5, 1901

Printed books will be cheap and abundant, and the art of illustrating and embellishing them will reach high perfection.

International difficulties will be settled by commissioners or conventions, instead of by appeal to arms to end in the destruction of life and property.

The Edward P. Allis Company, Milwaukee, about 1900.

Air ships will be a regular method of transportation, passengers from "fliers" being dropped to cities under the route by means of parachutes.

The habits of insect pests will be better understood, and their parasite enemies discovered and utilized so as to prevent destructive ravages upon vegetation.

It is estimated that the population of the United States in 2000 will be about 400,000,000, if the proportionate ratio of gain between 1800 and 1900 is maintained.

Photography in colors will be well understood and practiced, and the camera will contest with the type-setting machine in the manufacture of books and newspapers.

Utensils and dwellings will be manufactured largely of pulps and cements, so as to utilize vegetation and stone in every stage of decay, ordinary waste or unfitness.

The average crop of wheat per acre where planted, will be likely to rise from twelve to twenty bushels, as now, to 100 or more bushels per acre, to which all ground intensively cultivated is equal. There will be proportionate increase in all crops. Sugar will be an extensive northern product.

The clovers and other nitrogen-gathering plants and the bacteria which aid them in collecting this important element from the air, will both have been so bred as to enrich the earth with almost superabundance of the plant food which makes protein in plants and muscles and nerve in animals.

Scientific discoveries and appliances will do away with dangers to health incident to the massing of vast numbers in the cities. Water will be pure, temperature will be equalized, food will be scientifically prepared for use, and men and women will live longer by obeying the common sense laws of health.

Capital and labor will be at peace by the prevalence of the golden rule, which enjoins us to do to others as we would have them do to us. The working people, it is hoped, will all be shareholders, in the farm or factory where they work, and draw dividends from the profits. They will lose by all strikes, because the strike will be against their own interests.

By 2000 the phonographic principle will have been so perfected that the best books will appear in records or plates for use in many different styles of speaking machines. The exact tones of the elocutionist in speaking the words of the poet, teacher, philosopher and novelist will be reproduced in the library or parlor of every home. The exact tone of the sweet singer will also be faithfully reproduced.

The superior weapons of death made today will be exhibited in the museums of 2000 in contrast with clubs and other brutal instruments of war made by earlier races, of interest now to us, and observers will then wonder why their forefathers, who were endowed with the intelligence necessary to such marvelous mechanical skill, should still posses savage instincts and so thirst for the blood of those who may have offended their honor, that they are willing to shed their own.

The dress of the future—of the year 2000—will offer no resistance to free body action. This may involve a return to the garments of earlier times.

Fantastic Visions

While many observers based their predictions on current trends in science and technology, others offered more sweeping guesses. The first piece goes so far as to report the news of the future.

Wausau Pilot, January 22, 1901

The publishers of the *Cleveland World* recently issued a paper pur-
porting to give the news of Jan. 1, 2001. The phonetic system of
spelling is used throughout this alleged twenty-first century journal, and among the leading news articles are an account of the
opening of communication with Mars, a story of the robbery of
an airship express by bandits who froze the messenger to death
with liquid air, a description of the execution of a "murdres" by
vaporization and a recital of the discovery in the ruins of abandoned Cincinnati of several barrels containing a curious, foul
smelling liquid labeled beer. Minor items chronicle the intention
of "Mme. Sarah Heartburn" to make a farewell tour of America,
the death of a woman who once rocked George Washington to
sleep in his cradle and the fall of a workman from the ninety-sixth
floor of an office building.

> Arthur Palm, a fourteen-year-old Milwaukee student, published an article
> in his school newspaper depicting his vision of how America would look
> in the year 2001. Arthur took some of his futuristic ideas from an
> illustration in the January, 1901, issue of *Collier's Weekly* magazine, which
> appears on the facing page.

(Milwaukee) Excelsior, February, 1901

How it may appear a hundred years hence, when modern inventions have been carried to their highest point of development that
even Edison would feel jealous of the great inventions in the year
2001. In the year 2001 you will see sky-scrapers sticking far above
the clouds over 200 stories high. On the streets there will not be
any room for the street cars, so they will build lines way up in the
air, and there will be landings fastened to the high sky-scrapers,
where the people wait for the cars. The carlines will have different
kinds of names and you will see the name "Manhattan Air Line"
many hundreds of feet above the ground. You see air-ships and
carriages fastened to balloons for the transportation of the people
through the air, and you will often see collisions in the clouds. In
one of the sky-scrapers on the 119 story, you will see a sign, "Old
People Restored to Youth by Electricity, While You Wait." You will
see a tube stretched across the city called, "The United States Mail
Tube," and a sign called, The Wireless Telephone Local and European. There will be saloons in the large buildings and in the

Collier's Weekly, *January 12, 1901.*

window you will see the sign "Quick Lunch Compressed into Food Tablets." You may go to Europe in six hours by "The Submarine Line." The House-keepers will have an easy time; the dishes will be washed by electricity. In the year 2001, you will not see a single horse on Broadway, New York and only autos will be seen. In war the nations will have submarine torpedo boats which will destroy a whole fleet. In the year 2001, the locomotives will travel about 300 miles in an hour, but I think it is not necessary because, before you know it, you will be killed by a locomotive. The people of the Earth will be in close communication with Mars by being shot off in great cannons. The cannon ball will be hollow to contain food and drink.

4

"It Will Be a Glorious Century"

"Old Must Ever Fall Before the New"

While the tremendous scientific and technological advances of the nineteenth century inspired enthusiasm for the future, developments also led many to think about the changes that would occur in politics, economics, intellectual life, and religion. By the turn of the century, portents of things to come were already in the air. Organizations that called for change, such as labor unions, woman suffrage groups, and new political parties, had become prominent in the public eye. Writers at the turn of the century put forth new ideas about topics ranging from religion to education to diet. As the following article shows, the recent acquisition of the Philippines and Puerto Rico in the Spanish-American War and the annexation of Hawaii led some to speculate about how the nation's territorial boundaries might look in the future.

(Kenosha) Telegraph-Courier, January 10, 1901

What is in store for the United States in the present century? When the century just ended began, it was the comforting thought of the citizens of the new Republic that there stretched to the West and the North of them a limitless, trackless, unexplored domain that would be the abode of the hardy frontiersmen, the dwelling place of the rude pioneers for centuries to come. When the discoveries of [Robert] Gray and the explorations of Clark and Lewis laid open the vast undefined and unconfined West to the people of the United States and the rest of the world, the mind of man could not conceive the countless ages that should pass before that great expanse of territory would be the habitation of man and the home of thriving cities. The people of those days did not even dream of a time when steam transportation and telegraph and telephone should build up great cities on the very edge of the Western sea and bring the Columbia and the Pacific, vague realities in the minds of the men of the day, within speaking distance of the New England States. But all these things have come to pass, and within the comparatively short time of a little less than a century. Then what of the future?

Already those magnificent distances that completely baffled the conception of the fathers of the country have become all too short. Those broad expanses have become too confined, and those countless acres too few indeed for the rapidly growing population of the United States at the beginning of the twentieth century. Already it overflows the confines and reaches out for other fields. Its mighty progress cannot be staid. The genius of advancement that has so overleaped the bounds of all precedent in the last one hundred years cannot be restrained or contained within limits that it has already outgrown. Having brought under its mastery the tracts beyond the Mississippi and the Rockies, it will not pause at the brink of the sunny Pacific. But what is its goal? Hawaii and the islands of the Philippine archipelago were in its grasp before the cradle century of the nation had breathed its last. Next lie the areas of China with their seething populations. Is there room there for the children of the twentieth century? The old must ever fall before the new. The children of a decadent civilization cannot stand before the march of the offspring of regeneration. Either the creatures of the present day progress and civilization must dispossess the sons of the Orient, or, breathe new life into a decaying empire, and find employment for their energies in building a new nation from the ruins of an old.

> For many writers, progress meant the solution of problems that emerged during the nineteenth century. In Wisconsin, both socialist and progressive reformers addressed the problems of urban poverty and monopolies and insisted that only through fundamental change could America truly progress. The *Vorwärts* was the German-language organ of Milwaukee's Social-Democratic Party, and like Germans in the old country, it marked the turn of the century at the end of 1899 rather than 1900. Victor Berger, the paper's editor and the party's cofounder, most likely penned the editorial that follows. E. M. Scarola wrote the second piece, a poem entitled "The Child with Red Hair." Both items appear here in English translations from the original German.

(Milwaukee) Vorwärts, December 31, 1899

. . . If this century has been called (often falsely) the century of humanitarianism, the next will be called the century of radical social change, whether the changes be accomplished in a peaceful or bloody manner, gradually or suddenly. Socialism has begun its victory march through the civilized world, and nothing can stop its forward movement.

And yet we do not want to conceal the fact that monstrous difficulties must still be met before we can reach our proximate goal since a final goal for civilization does not exist. In this country the teachings of socialism are not understood by the great majority of the people, or else they are understood wrongly. And the difficulties do not come just from our open and direct opponents the capitalists but also from those who claim to have goals similar to our own.

WHi(X3)29507

A Milwaukee street, about 1909.

For the times are past when people could offer up notions like "property sharing" and "woman sharing" as socialist goals without appearing completely ridiculous in the eyes of reasonable people. But with this, the battle against socialist teachings has not been ended. On the one hand, capitalist reformers and proletarian demagogues steal socialism's own weapons and try to turn them against it. They take socialist slogans but give them a different meaning. Many of socialism's demands regarding municipalization or nationalization are accepted but brought into a context where they lose meaning and significance. On the other hand, a small band of orthodox believers claims the sole right to interpret socialism. It dismisses any actions taken to improve current conditions as purely a swindle; it persuades its followers to wait for the great "Crash-bang" and the "future state" and would gladly deliver those who disagree to the inquisition if it were possible. Thus, it is even more important than before that we Social-Democrats work against the falsification of democratic, scientific socialism by humbuggers as well as fanatics, that we offer in place of mere slogans insight into the real developments. This is doubly necessary in our Milwaukee, where the old capitalist parties have also appropriated certain socialist-sounding phrases and made good use of them at election time. . . . In the last two decades the conditions of earlier times in America have been completely stood on their heads: entirely new economic organizations such as the trusts have appeared, and the goals of the old political parties have been completely displaced. But on the other hand, despite crises, the capitalistic economic system has in no way taken on such an acute form that a catastrophe can be expected soon or in the foreseeable future. In short, given the ever new formations of economic life, the old demands, doctrines and proofs are in many cases insufficient; and, more than any socialist parties in other countries, American Social-Democrats have the mission of bringing clarity and ever more clarity about social conditions into the heads of the proletarians.

And that is one of the main missions of this newspaper: it stands for truth and clarity, even though many illusions and fond hopes may be destroyed thereby. For this newspaper is a mouthpiece for struggle; we struggle in all areas so that the producing classes—the workers and the farmers—may be raised to a higher level in the material, intellectual, moral, and physical sense; and this requires above all truth and clarity. These words should be the motto of Social-Democracy. . . .

We have great hopes for the new year, the year 1900. We expect intense and wide-ranging action. But we also expect great triumphs for the young Social-Democracy of America.

Here's to the new year!

(Milwaukee) Vorwärts, January 7, 1900

Mrs. Nineteen groans and moans and cries
and writhes with labor pains;
the "dignitaries of the nation" united
surround her childbirth bed.
She sees the cradle not far away
ready for the child, for her the funeral bier,
and she tears her clothes apart and cries out:
"The child will have red hair!"

Fright grips the circle of hypocrites,
the snobs and the parsons;
the blue coat quickly grabs his cudgel
and other "spiritual weapons."
The parson, from the pulpit,
incites his sheep to the altar:
Now you are damned! All of you.
"The child will have red hair!" . . .

Into your night our despair will sink,
the day is almost here;
our sunrise has arrived
and your stars are gone!
The morning song is already sounding,
the larks and the starling.
The snob is retreating! The parson fleeing!
"The child will have red hair!"

We are born free and equal,
we do not know oppression!
Hurray! You proletarian child!
You will give us equal rights!
The farmer—red! The bourgeoisie—red!
Ah, you changeable world!
Desperation is dead! The people have bread!
"The child will have red hair!"

Other newspapers offered a more moderate approach to progressive reform. John De Witt Warner, a former Democratic congressman from New York, outlined a number of progressive initiatives for urban reform in the following piece. It was published in translation in one of Milwaukee's German-language newspapers. The text printed here is taken from the original English-language version.

Milwaukee Herold und Seebote, January 1, 1901

In attempting to anticipate what "reforms" we may expect in municipal matters during the next century, experience warns us that, while in some details they may be so radical and novel as to make that name appropriate, they will, in the main, be such that they would be more accurately termed "developments."

Taking up at random the matters with which city authorities are now busy: Artificial light has for centuries been recognized as a necessity of civilized man and public order. It is, therefore, rapidly and certainly coming to be regarded as a want which should be directly met by the municipality; and it is as nearly certain as may be, first, that public control, and, in general, public operation of city light plants will prevail. And we are tending rapidly toward a similar policy as to heat.

As to transport facilities: not merely will clean, dry and spacious streets be the rule, but systems of subway transport will probably be more extensive than are now surface ones; while, both above and under ground, the rate of transport will be such as to approach a free supply. That is, fares will be so low, as compared with other factors in the use of cars, that these self-same factors, and not expense, will determine their use by each. It is probable that, as in the case of water, the expense of individual supply, so free as not to limit use, will be fully met by fares so petty as to be scarcely more than required to prevent waste; and the operation by the city of these "moving highways" will become as much a matter of course as is now the repair and preservation of our streets for pedestrians. The whole field of express service will be so extended as to provide not merely messenger service much more complete than now, but for the safe carriage and prompt delivery to any part of the municipality of articles deposited at any other part. Telephone service, also, will be correspondingly cheap and abundant.

One result of increased transport and communication facilities will be the growth of public kitchens, where shall be prepared the meals of most of our citizens, which they will receive ready served, of better quality, and more promptly and regularly, than the domestic economy of the average household can hope to furnish them. These will have been preceded by public laundries, which will relieve the wage earner's household of a most important item of its present discomforts.

It is not easy to predict how shall be solved the problem of manual labor by married women. Whether with better wages and cheaper living they will be in general relieved of other cares than those of wife and mother? or whether, with more of opportunity for self-support and partially relieved from present home duties, the number of wage earners among married women will increase? It is practically certain, however, that the right of every child to good care, nurture and education will be better protected with every decade; that day nurseries will be one of the public facilities soon provided as a matter of course; and that labor which takes mothers from their children will be permitted only in cases where proper care of all children below school age is definitely provided for.

Public baths so nearly free as to be habitually used by all and so numerous and extensive as to leave such use unlimited, will be as much a matter of course as sufficient air for breathing. Still greater relief, not merely to the poor, but especially to those of moderate and large means, will result from such a complete system of hospitals that, by 2000, for one who is so ill that he cannot go about, to remain at his residence will be as unusual as a hundred years since it was universal. In every considerable city, education, to the fullest extent of the capacity of its youth, will be literally free as air, and, up to what would now be considered a high standard, made quite compulsory in one way or another.

More provision will be made for public recreation. Beautiful sculpture, instructive paintings and fully equipped libraries will characterize the typical city.

And long before the year 2000 taxation will have been so adjusted as to encourage, not discourage, the fullest improvement of land; public franchises will be so universally operated direct by the public, that a street railway company or private water-works for public supply will seem as archaic as personal government by royal charter, or the farming of taxes.

Religious leaders figured prominently in the efforts to cure urban problems. In the following article, nationally syndicated columnist

Thomas DeWitt Talmage of Washington, D.C., devoted his weekly sermon to the topic of urban "redemption." Talmage's sermons were widely read throughout Wisconsin and were a weekly staple for twenty-nine years.

Elkhorn Blade, January 1, 1901

. . . Pulpit and printing press for the most part in our day are busy in discussing the condition of the cities at this time, but would it not be healthfully encouraging to all Christian workers and to all who are toiling to make the world better if we should this morning for a little while look forward to the time when our cities shall be revolutionized by the Gospel of the Son of God and all the darkness of sin and trouble and crime and suffering shall be gone from the sky, and it shall be "a morning without clouds?" . . .

I want you to understand, all you who are toiling for Christ, that the castles of sin are all going to be captured. The victory for Christ in these great towns is going to be so complete that not a man on earth or an angel in Heaven or a devil in hell will dispute it. How do I know? I know it just as certainly as God lives and that this is holy truth. The old Bible is full of it. The nation is to be saved. It makes a great difference with you and with me whether we are toiling on toward a defeat or toiling on toward a victory.

Now, in this municipal elevation of which I speak, I have to remark there will be greater financial prosperity than our cities have ever seen. Some people seem to have a morbid idea of the millennium, and they think when the better time comes to our cities and the world people will give their time up to psalm singing and the relating of their religious experience, and as all social life will be purified there will be no hilarity, and as all business will be purified there will be no enterprise. There is no ground for such an absurd anticipation. In the time of which I speak, where now one fortune is made there will be a hundred fortunes made. We all know business prosperity depends upon confidence between man and man. Now, when that time comes of which I speak, and all double dealing, all dishonesty and all fraud are gone out of commercial circles, thorough confidence will be established, and there will be better business done and larger fortunes gathered and mightier successes achieved.

The great business disasters of this country have come from the work of godless speculators and infamous stock gamblers. The great foe to business is crime. When the right shall have hurled back the wrong, and shall have purified the commercial code, and shall have thundered down fraudulent establishments, and shall have put into the hands of honest men the keys of business, blessed time for the bargain makers. I am not making a guess. I am telling you God's eternal truth. . . .

In that day of which I speak, do you believe that there will be any midnight carousal? Will there be any kicking off from marble steps of shivering mendicants? Will there be any unwashed, unfed, uncombed children? Will there be any blasphemies in the street? Will there be any inebriates staggering past? No. No wine stores, no lager beer saloons, no breweries where they make the three X's, no bloodshot eye, no bloated cheek, no instruments of ruin

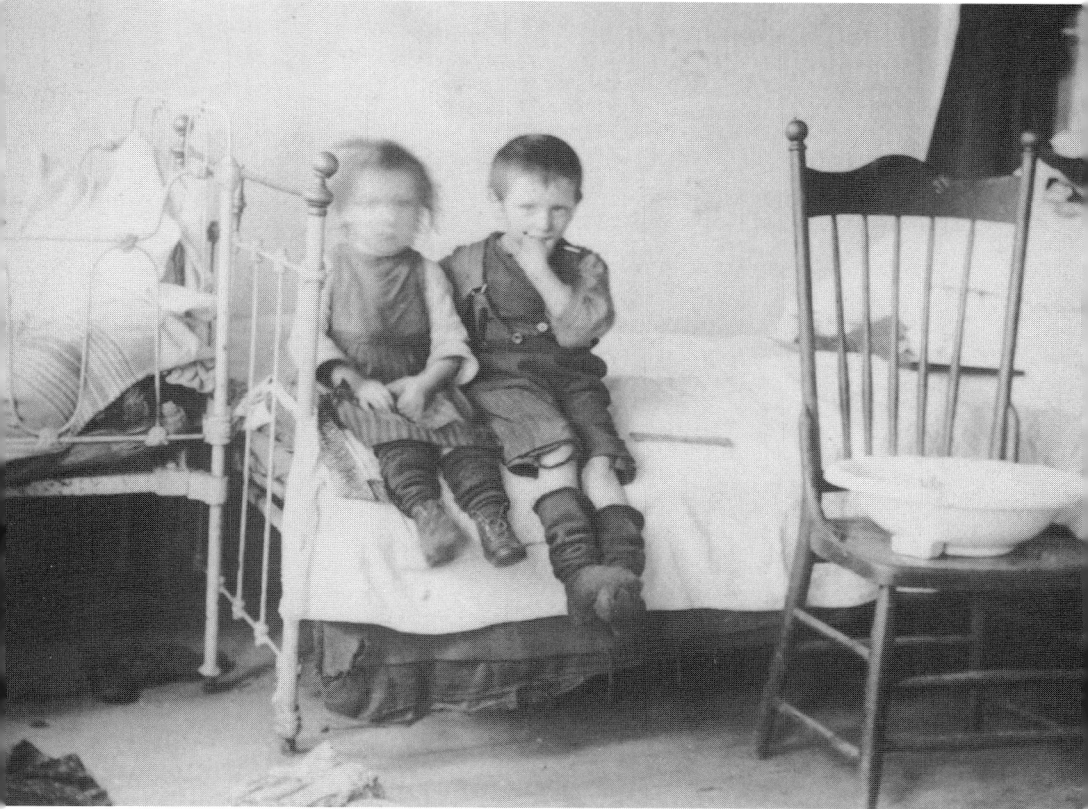

WHi(X3)29514

"In that day of which I speak. . . . [w]ill there be any unwashed, unfed, uncombed children?" Two Milwaukee children, 1909.

and destruction, no fist pounded forehead. The grandchildren of that woman who goes down the street with a curse, stoned by the boys that follow her, will be the reformers and the philanthropists and the Christian men and the honest merchants of our great cities.

God's love will yet bring back this ruined world to holiness and happiness. An Infinite Father bends over it in sympathy. And to the orphan He will be a Father, and to the widow He will be a husband, and to the outcast He will be a home, and to the poorest wretch that to-day crawls out of the ditch of his abominations, crying for mercy, He will be an all-pardoning Redeemer. The rocks will turn grey with age, the forests will be unmoored in the hurricane, the sun will shut its fiery eyelid, the stars will drop like blasted figs, the sea will heave its last groan and lash itself in expiring agony, the continents will drop like anchors in the deep, the world will wrap itself in sheet of flame and leap on the funeral pyre of the judgment day, but God's love will never die. It shall kindle its suns after all other lights have gone out. It will be a billowing sea after all other oceans have wept themselves away. It will warm itself by the blaze of a consuming world. It will sing while the archangel's trumpet peals, and the air is filled with the crash of breaking sepulchers, and the rush of the wings of the rising dead. Oh, commend that love to all the cities, and the morning without clouds will come! . . .

So you and I go forth, and all the people of God go forth, and they stretch their hand over the sea, the boiling sea of crime and sin and wretchedness. "It doesn't amount to anything," people say. Doesn't it? God's winds of help will after awhile begin to blow. A path will be cleared for the army of Christian philanthropists. The path will be lined with the treasures of Christian benevolence, and we will be greeted to the other beach by the clapping of all Heaven's cymbals, while those who pursued us and derided us and tried to destroy us will go down under the sea, and all that will be left of them will be cast high and dry upon the beach, the splintered wheel of a chariot or thrust out from the foam, the breathless nostril of a riderless charger.

Thoughts from the Street

The *Milwaukee Sentinel* asked a number of the city's citizens a common question: What is Milwaukee's greatest task in the twentieth century? Their answers reflected the diversity of viewpoints in Wisconsin's largest city.

Milwaukee Sentinel, December 30, 1900

John Johnston [cashier, Marine Midland Bank]—I think we are located to insure our becoming a large manufacturing center. Our climate is such that workmen can work a full day all year round, while in many localities, such as St. Louis, Cincinnati and elsewhere, the heat in the summer is so oppressive the workman cannot sleep at night and is not in condition to work the following day. It is invaluable to us that we have such a fine harbor on the chain of great lakes. We must keep our river so that we can admit the largest vessels. We must encourage manufacturers by not having more than a moderate rate of taxation; we must furnish them with cheap water and cheap light. . . .

Mrs. H. F. Whitcomb [wife of the president of Wisconsin Central Railroad]—Milwaukee's greatest task for the next century must be the proper education of children. First of all we must have adequate schools, especially in the kindergarten and primary grades, even if the High schools must be sacrificed to get this result. We must have the ungraded schools and the parental farm school in connection with the reformed system. We must also have the Juvenile Court law, and efficient probation officers to investigate every child's case thoroughly.

S. E. Tate [secretary, Swain and Tate Co.]—The thing that Milwaukee must have is a belt line. As matters are at present there are two railways here, one on the lake shore and the other in the Menomonee valley. This being the case, all manufactories must be located in these two limited districts, and just so far Milwaukee's progress will be impeded. By having a belt line we could have other roads touching Milwaukee. They would willingly come in then, affording us additional shipping facilities, and, what is more, provide more localities for manufacturing industries.

D. M. Schuler, Principal Eighth District School No. 2—What the city needs most of all in educational circles is more school room. This is a matter of present need, and might be considered building for the coming century. There should be more room, so as to give a more reasonable apportionment to the class teachers. Our teachers are woefully overcrowded, especially in the intermediate grades. I know of grades in which there are sixty-three pupils to the teacher, when there ought really to be fifty at most, while forty would be about the proper number that a teacher should be expected to take care of.

Ira B. Smith, President of Merchants and Manufacturers' Association—I should like to see seventy-six foot bridges at every street that crosses the rivers, making Milwaukee the Venice of America, and more railway facilities, and then Milwaukee will become a great commercial center.

E. A. Wadhams [president, Wadhams Oil and Grease Co.]—Not within 100 years, but immediately, we want boulevards connecting all the parks in the city, a viaduct from Twenty-seventh street to the south side and a lake drive to connect with the boulevards connecting with the park system.

E. L. Philipp [Milwaukee businessman and future Republican governor]—What do we need most during the next century? Why, a Republican administration, to begin as soon as possible and remain in charge indefinitely. We want good, honest men at the head of our affairs, and with such we need have no fear concerning the city's progress during the next 100 years.

Henry J. Baumgaertner [Republican nominee for mayor, 1900]—The city is most in need of a larger percentage of citizens who do their own thinking; of men who dare to assert their rights and manhood, and whose actions are not wholly controlled by an interested few, for pecuniary gain. Then all other city needs, such as municipal ownership of public utilities, more adequate railway facilities, just taxation, etc., will follow as a matter of course, in rapid succession, and the year 2000 will dawn upon Milwaukee with a population twentyfold that of to-day.

Matt J. Simpelaar [superintendent, Edward Keogh Press]—What our fast growing manufacturing city needs most in this era of great industrial development and general prosperity is a centrally located official employment bureau. I have in mind a public office in the city hall where a systematic daily bulletin should be kept of all employers of labor of any kind in need of hands; a place where a person in search of work could register, and make a daily call to see if there was any demand for help in his vocation. This bulletin of firms in need of help I would have published daily in the official city paper, besides being kept prominently on a blackboard in the office. I believe it would be a step in the right direction and prove of great benefit to employers as well as the working classes. There are no doubt, many employers to-day looking for the right person, as well as willing and able hands looking for work, while both necessarily are ignorant of each other's wants. We keep a very systematic and elaborate record of births, deaths and marriages, and of people in jails and prisons. Why not pay a little more attention to the real live condition of our social structure? I feel sure that a public office, systematically conducted, free from all expense to the person in need of its information in hand, would materially diminish the population of that public factory known as the house of correction.

Under-Sheriff Louis Meyer—To secure a new place for boy criminals is one of the things that must be undertaken—the quicker the better.

Ignatz Czerwinski [real estate developer]—A larger influx of European immigration is needed. We want more factories, and the prosperity which will accompany them.

Deputy Comptroller George W. Porth—One of the tasks the city must accomplish is the reduction of taxes. How? More economy in all city departments. We must construct more schools; and we need deeper river channels.

Ald. Henry Smith—Social Revolution! It's got to come. You can't get away from it. It's either coming or we will have slavery. And when it comes there will be wisdom in city government and all faults of to-day will be met! Public ownership of public utilities also must be accomplished.

C. B. Willis, General Secretary of the Y.M.C.A.—What the city needs is righteous men: men who fear God and keep His commandments. We would then have no difficulty with municipal corruption or any other.

"The Best Dairy State in the Union"

In 1900 Wisconsin was still overwhelmingly rural, and dairying was the backbone of the state's agricultural economy. In the following articles, prominent state figures offer their visions of Wisconsin dairying in the twentieth century. Henry Cullen Adams, state dairy food commissioner, wrote the first article. Adams strongly supported the pending "Grout bill" in Congress which sought to ban oleomargarine colored to look like butter. William Dempster Hoard, former governor and publisher of *Hoard's Dairyman* magazine, wrote the second piece.

Milwaukee Sentinel, December 30, 1900

Dairying is Wisconsin's greatest agricultural interest. Our cheese factories produce 45,000,000 pounds of cheddar and 15,000,000 pounds of Swiss, Limberger and other kinds of cheese each year. Our creameries and private dairies have an annual product of

A foot-powered milking machine, 1901.

80,000,000 pounds of butter. Our pastures and fields support 1,000,000 cows that yield an annual revenue of $35,000,000.

We are progressing rapidly toward still larger and better results. More farmers are doing more and better thinking every year. As in every other industry, invention is cheapening the cost and improving the character of the product. The old tin milk pan is a memory. The marvelous separator that skims milk with lightning speed by steam or hand power is a living and profitable reality. The dash churn, that old-fashioned instrument of torture, has been displaced by modern machines run by dogs and sheep, by steam and electricity. Refrigerator cars carry fresh Wisconsin butter into the markets of Memphis and New Orleans. The cow herself is more respectable than ten years ago because she is better bred. The future has no greater possibilities in Wisconsin dairying than in the line of breeding good dairy stock. The cow that does not pay and cannot be made to pay is still common in this state. The future, with the universal education which it will bring to dairymen, will destroy her. It will breed "general purpose" nonsense out of dairy cows and will breed cream into milk and color into butter. It will breed as its best type that cow which has no waste bone or flesh, which has tremendous digestive capacity and power to elaborate food into good milk. In other words makes a cow machine which will make the most butter fat from a given amount of raw material. The future will bring clean milk and cream into every market in the state.

Absolute dairy cleanliness and pasteurization of milk and the products will be secured by state and municipal laws, which shall provide ample agencies for enforcement.

Barns lighted by electricity, well-ventilated and clean will protect our dairy cows from summer storms and winter's cold. The silo will give canned green fodder to give summer succulence to the winter ration upon every dairy farm. The science and art of feeding will be universally understood and protein and carbohydrates will go into cows in right proportion.

All of our butter will have good grain, rich flavor and the color that nature gives. Our American cheese will be placed upon the market only when well cured and rich in butter fat. Our Limberger cheese will be more redolent than ever with those odors which become better as they grow worse.

The dairyman of the future will do business in a home where flowers bloom and comfort reigns. Where the laws of sanitation in construction will be carefully regarded, where a good share of the world's knowledge as found in papers and magazines and books shall have a place, where a telephone will connect him with neighbors and markets, where children will be taught by surroundings and the example of clean and prosperous life to love the farm and to so live that their good citizenship shall serve the state. The future will see Northern Wisconsin dotted with creameries and cheese factories. The cow will follow the axe with an industry as enduring as time. She will be a gold mine and a blessing in every agricultural community. Her army of a million will grow to millions, that within half a century will yield the state a revenue of $100,000,000 a year. Our domestic markets will grow with our population, and per capita consumption will increase with improved quality of product.

In the coming century, we will break into the trade of the Orient with our dairy products. We will teach the Chinese to eat butter instead of bugs. The "Yellow Peril" will disappear under the Christianizing influences of the product of the American cow. The Grout bill will become a law. Oleomargarine will wear its own uniform of white or go to the lockup. The cow will chew her cud serene in her comfort, beautiful in her form, unrivaled in her usefulness, and Wisconsin will continue to be what it now is, the best dairy state in the Union.

Milwaukee Sentinel, December 30, 1900

You ask for a brief statement of my opinion concerning the future of the dairy industry in Wisconsin. I would reply that in my opinion the state has a bright future before it in this particular, provided its people look at the question in a right light. Wisconsin occupies already a foremost position among all the states of the Union in regard to the extent and quality of its dairy product and in particular for what it is doing for advanced dairy education among the farmers. It has the strongest dairy school in the nation. Its agricultural college is doing more than any similar institution to educate the youth of the farm to a right understanding of what it means to be a successful dairy farmer. Its State Dairymen's association is one of the strongest in the Union, and has kept instructors in the field for years who travel among the cheese factories and creameries and give instruction to the operators as to the latest and best methods of butter and cheese making. They also hold meetings among the patrons and discuss the proper methods for caring for the milk and milk utensils, as well as the proper management of cows.

Its farm institutes, 100 in number, dispense a vast amount of useful information concerning the most successful methods of dairy farm management, and the breeding and feeding and handling of dairy cattle.

Nowhere in the Union is the thought, purpose and action of the farmers better organized on this great branch of agriculture than in Wisconsin.

We have a very efficient Dairy and Food commission, with excellent laws for the protection of dairy products.

I believe the census of 1900 will show that the milk product of Wisconsin will exceed $40,000,000 in value.

Northern Wisconsin, an empire almost in extent, bids fair to become a theater of production for the finest butter and cheese on the continent. Its stable temperature in summer, its great productiveness in all of the grasses and its unexcelled water, all point to a magnificent future for the dairy industry in that portion of the state. All the cow will ask at the hands of the people of Wisconsin is a fair show against all frauds and counterfeits, and she will in a few years bring unexampled wealth and prosperity to the state.

Every man in the state be he farmer, lumberman, manufacturer or mechanic should feel a loyal patriotic pride in the building up of so magnificent an industry. There need be no fears that the business will be overdone, provided the cow can have the market to herself. From 1880 to 1881 there was one cow to 4½ people; from 1885 to 1890 one cow to 4 people; from 1890 to 1895 one to 4.80, and from 1895 to 1900 one cow to 5.33. The market statistics for the same length of time show a steady decline in the price of butter. The average for the first period was 29.33 cents; the second period 26.23 cents; the third period 24.09 cents; the fourth period 19.24 cents. Yet owing to the growth in the knowledge of dairy economics, the farmer of to-day, if he will make himself intelligent, can produce butter and cheese at better profit than he could fifteen years ago. This condition has come about through a manifest improvement of the dairy capacity of our cows, more intelligent ideas of feeding and a better understanding of how and what to grow as food crops for dairy cattle.

Wisconsin ought of right, to be the foremost state in the Union in the production of all breeds of dairy cattle. It has splendid opportunity in this direction if only its most intelligent and wealthy farmers will but take advantage of the reputation the state now enjoys as a great center of dairy activity. We need a thousand first-class breeders of Jersey, Guernsey, Holstein and Ayrshire cattle. This state should be as famous for its thoroughbred dairy cattle as Kentucky is for its horses. The demand is world wide and Wisconsin enterprise and brain should meet it.

As the old growth forests of northern Wisconsin fell before the lumberman's ax, many boosters sought to convince immigrants of the agricultural promise of this thinly populated Cutover district. Former Wisconsin governor William Upham predicted a bright future for farmers in this part of the state.

Milwaukee Sentinel, December 30, 1900

The future of Northern Wisconsin is in the hands of the agriculturist. As Joseph Cook says in one of his lectures, "a country of 'Wetness' is a country of 'Fatness.' "

Pulling stumps on the Christopher Paustenbach farm,
east of Medford, Taylor County, 1895.

We certainly have the "wetness" which means grass and it only requires the hand of man to place his herds of cattle and flocks of sheep upon the lands in Northern Wisconsin to make this country rich. The timber is rapidly being converted into lumber and its various products. Pine is obsolete upon the line of the railroads. The hemlock is being rapidly cut and the land followed up by the farmers, will make Northern Wisconsin as wealthy and productive as any portion of our great and beautiful state.

A World of Ideas

In addition to stories about the future of urban and rural life, newspaper readers encountered articles that predicted significant intellectual progress. In the following piece, Professor Albert Ross Parsons, president of the American College of Musicians in New York, offers his views on the future of music in the coming century. The second article offers a glimpse into the future of American literature.

Superior Evening Telegram, January 10, 1901

. . . The twentieth century will witness in America an unparalleled extension of musical enlightenment. With a steady increase of orchestral, choral and solo performances of the greatest music by traveling orchestras and artists of world-renowned excellence, and resulting growth of local musical organizations and societies of many sorts; with an enormous increase in manufacture of musical instruments and the publication of good music of all types and eras; with hundreds of thousands of more or less serious students of music; and with the introduction into the homes of the nation of marvelous automatic devices of American invention for rendering the greatest music familiar as household words, independently of the agency of laboriously acquired technique, public musical taste and appreciation cannot fast to become extraordinarily improved; and with the simplest to the most complex will have to reach a certain standard of quality in order to enjoy any sort of popularity. It has already become hard for any one but a composer of talent and training to secure a commission to write the music for even the lightest of operettas, and good composers are more in demand than ever before to supply incidental music for the theatre. . . .

Kenosha Evening News, January 4, 1901

It has been the unanimous verdict of the critics that no holiday season has produced so many readable books in the line of fiction and biographical history as the last. It is indubitable that the product has been voluminous beyond precedent, and probably the judgment of the people, who are in reality in the end the arbiters of an author's fate, would sustain the critics. With it conceded that the quantity of books written by American authors and the quality of the work are both superior to former years of the latter half of the century, one is inclined to speculate some on the future of literature in this country.

It is a fact that every American notes with regret and a little mortification, perhaps, that among the authorized lists of the greatest authors and their works of the past century, the United States is either altogether overlooked or only very meagerly represented. Among those whom the critics are going to let live are, among the writers of fiction, such names as Balzac and Dumas, of France, Thackeray and Dickens, of England, and Scott, beside Stevenson and Kipling. Among the poets are Byron, Tennyson, Swineburne, Wordsworth, Hugo, De Mussey, Heine, Goethe and Pushkin. Among the historians are Macaulay, Mommsen, Ranke, Taine, Carlyle and Thiers. Where are the Americans? Occasionally some lone critic will find a place among the writers of fiction for Hawthorne and Cooper, and among the poets for Holmes and Lowell. Emerson and Fiske are also mentioned at times, but they are all usually spoken of as among those less fortunate ones whose writings, though loved by their contemporaries, will not be able to endure the test of time.

If the beacon lights of American literature are all undeserving of a niche in the hall of fame, what are the prospects for the twentieth century? If Hawthorne and Cooper and Lowell and Emerson are doomed to "pale their ineffectual light" in the mists of the coming years, what of the men and women who are at present representing the United States in the literary arena? The writers of the old school are almost passed away. Holmes lived to be as he wrote, "The last leaf on the tree," and Howells is practically the only survivor of the galaxy of literary stars that formerly shone in the diadem of American literature. New writers are taking the places of the old and the new century begins with an entirely new coterie of aspirants struggling for literary honors unattained or abandoned by those who have gone before.

What the prospects are, those best able to judge are too reticent to hazard. It is probably safe to say that the younger writers of the United States have kept pace with the younger writers of other countries, with the possible exception of England, and Page, Grant, Harland and Bachellier have been well received by the public and credited by the critics with quite an unusual degree of talent. What, if they are allowed to live, these authors will achieve is entirely a matter of conjecture. As yet no latter day author has sprung into life with that immortal spark aglow in his lines that seems to betoken another Thackeray or Dickens, or even another Hawthorne. Whatever else may be said of the twentieth century, it may certainly be ventured that in the first years, at least, there will be no dearth of new and fresh reading, whatever may be said of the quality of the work and its effect upon the literature of the country and the thought of the age.

An excellent educational system fed optimism for the future of Wisconsin. State and local officials strove to improve methods of teaching at all levels and saw great hope in the state's ability to meet the educational needs of its youth. The following article was drawn from the annual address of Wisconsin Teachers' Association's Acting President W. H. Elson, entitled "The Necessity for Stimulating and Utilizing Purpose in School Work."

Milwaukee Sentinel, December 29, 1899

. . . The nineteenth century school leads the child to information; it leads him to repeat information; it stimulates only or chiefly the gathering-in process; it fosters the spirit of self-accumulation; it breeds selfishness. On the contrary the twentieth century school, with a clearer insight and a fuller recognition of the fundamental law of growth, will lead the child to use his acquisitions in new fields of endeavor; it will lead him to put forth, to express, to achieve by doing; it will bless him with the joy of achievement; it will breed consecration, devotion, benevolence in a helpful service to others; from a tendency to self-preservation it will lead him into a life of self-assertion; from a tendency to self-accumulation it will lead him into channels of altruism. The nineteenth century school lays more stress on the inleading currents than on the outleading currents; more on the sensory system than on the motor system; more on the impressive activities than on the expressive activities; more on the absorbing process and on the receptive attitude than on the productive and creative tendencies; more on the acquisition of knowledge than on the use of it. The twentieth century school will adjust and equalize the emphasis; it will concern itself with what the child knows that he can use, with what he can do, with what he measures in terms of life-efficiency; it will enquire what power he has to solve new problems, to adjust means to end, to measure action to possible result.

Two significant facts are apparent in the modern movement in education. First, the growing tendency and effort to base all school work on the child's experience and to enlarge and enrich this experience. Second, the growing tendency to provide for the completion of mental acts in actual achievement. The development of the arts and sciences has put into active service in the conditions of modern living a wealth of material which it is the business of the school to utilize in cultivating a spirit of inquiry and investigation, and a habit of relating all knowledge to practical life-purposes. The larger use of observation and experiment which now forms a part of the daily work of all schools calls for the larger use of the hand in constructive doing. Experience must always look to achievement for its justification. Progress in educational practice is measured, not by advancement in one or the other of these lines, but in their close correlation in purpose. The child is to gain knowledge at first hand from personal experience, but he is also to develop power to use knowledge thus gained. What schools must need is the vitalizing touch that purpose gives. When observation and experiment beget in the child the habit of relating all new income to new fields of achievement then purpose has been stimulated and proper correlation has been made between acquisition and expression, between thought and action. If half the time and energy spent within the past few years in attempting to make forced and mechanical correlations between one thought- subject and another and in attempting to determine the proper and exact number of correlating centers—whether there should be one, or three, or five—had been spent in expanding the field of reactive conduct, and providing for a close correlation between seeing and doing, between observation and expressing, fewer children would have gone to wreck in the meantime and the cause of education would have been greatly helped. This is said with a full measure of appreciation of the rich contribution which the study of correlation in the past few years has brought to the elementary school. . . .

> In the following piece, James H. Stout of Menomonie, a state senator
> and philanthropist who founded Stout Training School, which later
> became the University of Wisconsin-Stout, speculated on future
> directions in university education.

Milwaukee Sentinel, December 30, 1900

I am asked to state for *The Sentinel* the lines along which I think university education is likely to be developed in the coming years. The development of universities in the immediate future will be the outcome of their history in the past and the greatest and future demands of students seeking higher education.

The most significant changes in university education during the past twenty-five years seem to me to have been the following:

1. The introduction of the laboratory and the seminary methods of instruction.
2. The enlargement of the university curriculum by the introduction of the study of science, and later of history, economics and allied subjects.
3. The enlargement of the scope of university instruction by the addition of graduate study.
4. The development and extension of technical courses.

University of Wisconsin biology laboratory, 1899.

The first introduction of all of these changes must be dated considerably farther back than a quarter of a century, but their existence in universities as active and powerful educational forces is scarcely longer than twenty-five years. It is hardly probable that the first quarter of the twentieth century will witness new movements and changes in university education as important and extensive as these. The work of the years immediately before us will be to carry forward the movements already initiated. The enrichment and enlargement of the university curricula came as a response to the pressure exerted by the general intellectual movement of the world in the generation just past. While new sciences will be introduced into the curriculum and the teaching of history and of politics will be greatly extended, it is hardly possible that new fields for investigation will be opened at all comparable to those covered by these great departments of thought,—the one pertaining to the world and the other to society. It is probable that the necessities of the community will lead to a differentiation in the teaching of these subjects and that, on the one hand, both science and history will be taught to certain classes on account of their value as a means of general culture, and that, in other directions, the teaching will be specialized as a means of technical training.

Undoubtedly the fact of most immediate practical significance in higher education is the enormous increase in the demand for technical education. Increase in population, leading to a great growth in the size of the communities, and the resulting complexity and intensity of social life, makes great and increasing demands for special training. This is especially true in engineering. There is now a demand for technically trained engineers in very numerous directions where but a few years ago no openings existed for persons so trained, and, so far as the future can be forecast, the field for the engineer will be very rapidly enlarged during the years immediately before us. The same demand for technical training is present in other directions. Only a very few years ago there was no demand for technical training for those engaged in agriculture, but in all parts of the country this demand is now great, and rapidly increasing, and technical agricultural instruction will form an important part of the education of the future. The more specialized departments of commerce are now beginning to demand a similar technical training, and as commerce extends and specializes, as it is sure to do, this demand will be great and will have to be met by the multiplication and development of the new courses of study now just established in a few universities. Training for public service is a department of technical education about which much has been said, but for which there can scarcely be said to exist a general demand at the present time. Undoubtedly, however, as necessity forces our communities to administer their public affairs from the standpoint of business and not of politics, a great demand will arise for men trained for this branch of service.

This increase in demand for technical education does not mean a decrease in the demand for general education. On the contrary, all signs indicate that the coming years will see a great increase in this demand, both as regards the number of persons seeking a higher education and in the amount and quality of the education which is required. The most significant symptom of this movement is shown by the development of the graduate departments in our universities and the great increase in the number of persons seeking such instruction. At present there are about 2,500 graduate students in the thirteen largest institutions in this country, while twenty-five years ago graduate work had hardly begun. This extension of the undergraduate courses means that there are many persons who feel that the four years of a college course is too short a time for them to learn all they wish and need to know of the enlarged curriculum which the colleges are offering, and also means that in many departments, such as teaching, a greater amount of training is demanded than can be supplied by the undergraduate course.

The undergraduate course will be sought in the future by a constantly increasing number of students as a preparation for higher professional study. Twenty-five years ago very few persons in the West were pursuing an undergraduate course as a preparation for the study of medicine or law, while to-day the number of persons in every college who are looking to one or the other of these professions is great and is rapidly growing. Still further, as the community enlarges there will be a larger number of students who will come to universities for a liberal education without expectation of directly using this in business or professional life, and who will call upon the universities for courses of liberal culture in language and literature, science, history and other departments of learning and thought.

If then I should sum up what seems to me the probable trend of university development during the coming years, I should look for it in the directions of a rapid increase in graduate instruction and in the number of graduate students and in the technical departments. Coordinate with this increase I should expect a progressive enrichment of the general undergraduate curricula of the universities and constant improvements in their methods. I do not expect, however, to see in the university of the future any such educational revolutions as those which have been brought about by the introduction of the laboratory and seminary methods. University development during the next generation will be a growth rather than a revolution.

"Knowledge Is Power, Especially in the Kitchen"

Sarah Tyson Rorer, an author, editor, and lecturer from Philadelphia, offered a visionary look at the future of diet, health, and kitchen technology, illustrating the close ties binding technology and education to social change.

(Superior) Leader-Clarion, January 4, 1901

In the new century the fact will gradually be made clearer to men and women that it is much more sensible for them to eat to live than to live to eat. With the advent of the educated cook and the intelligent housekeeper we shall learn more about the right food for different persons, said Mrs. Sarah Tyson Rorer to a Philadelphia Press reporter. By the educated cook I mean the one who, especially trained for this branch of woman's work, must surely in the near future take the place of the ignorant woman in the kitchen.

The girls in our cooking schools and public schools who are taking the trouble now to learn the right principles of cooking will reap their reward. They will be masters of the situation, not servants of their servants. The general to be a perfect commander must thoroughly understand the tactics of the private. Knowledge is power, especially in the kitchen.

WHi(X3)26295

A Wisconsin kitchen at the turn of the century.

The man of the house when he wants a competent clerk takes infinite pains to get him. When he finds the right man, he has no hesitation in paying him his price. The woman of the house goes to an intelligence office and often more from necessity than from choice employs an inexpensive woman for her kitchen who is totally ignorant of every possible principle belonging to its management. If the man of the house only knew it, the woman in the kitchen is of far more importance to the health and the happiness of himself and his family than the man in his office.

The men and women who are to do the important work of the coming century will eat less meat. Vegetarianism has acquired a stride that no cry of fanaticism from prejudiced meat eaters can possibly check. The growth of vegetarianism means the disappearance of the ignorant cook. Much greater care must be given to vegetable than to meat cookery. Water soaked vegetables are not appetizing or sightly. The woman from the "intelligence" office usually knows enough to take a piece of meat, even of the poorer quality, put it on the stove, get up a fierce blaze and produce something fairly fit for the table.

But what does she do with vegetables? Simply ruins them. She boils them at a gallop, dissolves all their flavor and pours it without flinching down the drain. Then she dishes up the woody fiber and seasons it liberally with salt and pepper. If one wants the flavor of "tasty" vegetables and good coffee under such management, go to the top of the house. They are there, and there they stay if one has draperies. Badly cooked vegetables are absolutely devoid of nourishment and prime promoters of indigestion. The men and women of the twentieth century are not going to put up with these blunders. In fact, they cannot do so and live. The educated cook must come.

The properly regulated kitchen which I see in the near future will have no use for coal. The cook who wants to prepare a dainty and nourishing table would rather have her coal burned a long distance from her kitchen and supplied to her through pipes in the form of gas. I am not enough of a mechanic to discuss the probable utility of electrical stoves, but I do not think that they will ever prove much of a factor in the kitchen. Special electrical appliances to lessen labor in the kitchen may be more or less useful, but gas will be the cooking fuel for a very long time to come.

In the new century kitchen a thermometer will occupy a conspicuous place on the shelf.

As time goes on the dinner table will be made more attractive by pretty lamp shades and dainty flowers and ferns. It will appeal to the eye as well as to the palate. In satisfying their appetites men will drift more into the idea of esoteric Buddhism. The coarser forms of food will disappear. Less time will be spent in preparing dishes that have no value as nourishment. The woman who has no ideas of household economy beyond making an attractive but indigestible layer cake will be eliminated.

"Will Lovely Women Do the Proposing?"

At the turn of the century, although women still lacked the vote, many observers expressed a great deal of optimism for the "twentieth-century woman." Yet they sometimes differed as to what social changes would occur. In the following two articles, the authors offer very different perspectives on the future of women and social roles. The first article is a continuation of the piece by Gertrude Thayer begun on page 68.

Janesville Daily Gazette, January 4, 1901

. . . Here are a few things, for instance, which she expects to gain by the end of the twentieth century:

She is going to vote.

She is going to insist that she shall be paid the same wages as men for an equal amount of work.

She will have the same privileges as a man after her day's labor.

She will be able to go alone to the theater and restaurant without the painful necessity of dragging a man with her. When this is brought about, men will find themselves much less sought after.

When the nerves of her employer become a trifle on edge and he lights a cigarette to soothe them, she may give herself the same comfort if she chooses. The fact that she ought not to smoke because she is a woman will seem a humorous rather than a logical point of view.

When she marries a man and she is the larger wage earner, she will be the head of the house.

Her clothes will be comfortable as well as artistic.

She will hold any or every office where political integrity is demanded.

In fact should matters become too bad she wouldn't mind becoming president of the United States.

WHi(X3)N2904

*Woman suffrage activists, about 1903. Kneeling at far right is
Ada James, a suffrage leader from Richland Center.*

Platteville Journal, January 11, 1901

In the Twentieth century—
    Will lovely women do the proposing?
    Will woman bosses run politics as they now run the home?
    Will men wear birds on their hats and crochet?
    Will the housemaid be a houseman?
    Will horses be exhibited as curiosities?
    Will politics be run on a philanthropic basis?
    Will the Boston woman discover the north pole?
    Will little airships be provided for messenger boys?
    Will men wear frilled shirt waists and women trousers?
    Will the estimable Mrs. Grundy be driven to a convent?
    Will the college girl carry a cane and smoke a pipe?
    Will there be free lunch stands for women?
    Will men go to church evenings instead of to the club?
    Will the wife kiss her husband good-bye before starting off to
business?
    Will women either wear short skirts or have pages to carry their
trains?

Will squirrels wait just a quarter of a second longer to make faces at the hunter?

Will rich noblemen marry poor American girls?

Will hornets and other stinging things arbitrate instead of fight when their nests are pulled?

Will the grain be extracted from the heads of wheat and other cereals by a magnet and save the labor of harvesting straw?

Will there be a law compelling barbers to remain silent?

Will cows come home at milking time as eagerly as field hands come to supper?

And will those same cows semioccasionally turn grass into butter instead of milk?

Will there be any escape from the coon song save suicide?

Will every busy man wear an illuminated collar button?

Will mind reading furnish a key to the intentions of hens as to their duties and villainies?

Will the automatic principle be adjusted to taxes so that they pay themselves?

Will there be a society for the extermination of noisy milkmen which will really exterminate?

Will pounds be pounds and quarts be quarts in weight as well as in price?

Will women be compelled to flatten their pompadours at the theater so that men may see the play?

Will all consumers of anthracite have the common sense to lay in their winter stock in midsummer at any sacrifice?

Will the creatures that build guano mountains at the equator occasionally fly over the impoverished farms of North America?

Will our beloved country still be going to the "demnition bo-wwows" and political orators howling for votes to save it?

Now, candidly, wouldn't you like to know what sayers will be saying, thinkers thinking, writers writing, doers doing and plotters plotting at the end of the next hundred years?

"Christians Will Draw Nearer Together"

Many religious leaders looked to the new century with optimism. The following two articles summarize sermons by two such clergymen. In the first sermon, Rev. Lewis Keller of the Pilgrim Congregational Church in Milwaukee discusses the importance of spreading the influence of American Christianity throughout the world.

Milwaukee Sentinel, December 31, 1900

"We have become a world power and have set sail to take our proper position in the work of evangelizing the Orient," declared the Rev. L. H. Keller in a sermon on "The Message of the Old Century to the New" at Pilgrim Congregational church last night. "It is our duty to civilize and Christianize these half-wild peoples. Our missionary problem is one of the most important of all that confront us on the threshhold of the new century." At another point in his discourse Mr. Keller said: "Competition is a thing of the past. Trusts have come in obedience to economic laws and they will remain. They may abuse their powers, but they are here to stay and the people will keep them in check." The message of the new century, Mr. Keller said, was one of congratulation for the marvelous achievements of the past hundred years and the promise of similar wonders for the coming centurial cycle. It also bore a message of congratulation for the world-wide fellowship existing. Among the bequests of the old to the new century, Mr. Keller mentioned a number of scientific discoveries and inventions, and the establishment of such world-wide organizations as the Y.M.C.A., W.C.T.U., Christian Endeavor, Red Cross, Sunday school, international postal and cable systems and international bureau of weights and measures. He declared that it was a source of gratification to know that the membership of the Evangelical churches had increased three times as fast as that of the Catholic church during the same period. He used as his text the Ninety-fourth psalm, "A thousand years in Thy sight are but as yesterday."

> The article below describes a sermon given by George Ide at the Grand Avenue Church in Milwaukee. In the sermon, Ide refers to Dr. John Dowie, founder of the Christian Catholic Church in Chicago and a healing evangelist.

Milwaukee Sentinel, January 8, 1900

That the religion of the twentieth century will be one in which denominationalism will be nearly or quite evolved out of existence was the ground taken by Dr. George Ide in his sermon at the Grand Avenue Congregational church yesterday morning on "What Is to Be the Characteristic of the Twentieth Century Religion?" In the religion which will be predominant in the hundred years to come, there will be no religious fads, Dr. Ide held, and there will be no radical stand taken in behalf of the Apostolic Succession, of the premillennial advent of Christ, or of Christian science.

When a church devotes its attention to the fostering of "isms," it was devoting itself to the propagation of a specialty, the pastor said. The heathen religions developed men along only special lines, and the early history of the Christian church had the same fault. After nineteen centuries of development, however, the theologists were beginning to realize that the specialty of Christianity should be that it has no specialty but was a general broadener of man's talents.

Dr. Ide said that in his estimation we were already in the beginning of a new century and that those who thought themselves at the last of the nineteenth century will "find themselves at the rear of the procession" eventually. The ancient world was a compendium of specialities, in religions, social condition and the like. The Persian, Egyptian and the Buddhist religions were all specialties, as that of the Egyptians was essentially the caring for the dead. While their religions were already extinct the Christian religion was growing more and more to realize that its characteristic was love, and in love there were no specialties, as it had no bounds or directions. Some one might say that "We are the church," said Dr. Ide, "as our church runs straight back and is in line with the Apostolic Succession." The more this point was insisted upon the further away from the intent of Christ's religion would that church be. Denominationalism had not now the strong hold upon the churches that it once had. That meant that they were getting away from their specialities, not that they were losing their special forms of organization, as possibly they ought not to do.

To insist upon the doctrine of the premillennial advent of Christ, not to argue as to the truth of the doctrine, is to divert the church from the mission for which it was intended. To say that Christianity must not be applied to politics, learning and to the every day affairs of life was a conception of Christianity, Dr. Ide contended, that was passing and would not be heard of after the twentieth century.

"In the course of a conversation the other day," said Dr. Ide, "I asked a man what church he belonged to. He said he belonged to Dr. Dowie's church. He said that Dr. Dowie was a wonderful man. He has bought several thousand acres of land and we are going to build a city and we shall have a delightful community. The peculiar feature of that city would be that there would be no doctors in it. Here is an attempt to dwarf and minimize Christianity into a specialty, and to make the main issue consist in Faith-cure. The whole movement gathers about this one idea; remove that, and there would be nothing left of the movement. Christian Science belongs to the same class of spurious notions concerning Christianity. This is the point: if it could be shown, or if it were admitted by the Christian Scientists themselves, that sickness is a real thing, and not an imaginary thing, there would be nothing left of the whole scheme and it would evaporate into thin air."

"I believe that we have entered upon an era of men-making rather than the cultivation of 'fads,' and that the church will be known in the future, not by certain formulae of doctrine, however important in themselves, but by its success in transforming men into the likeness of Christ. What the world needs first is men, not specialists. Get your man and then put him anywhere, in the legal profession or in the home, and everything which he does will wear the marks and express the quality of that transformation which has taken place in his life."

> Not all predictions for the future of religion were optimistic. Citing the pessimism of Bishop Henry Potter of New York and English philosopher John Watson, this editorial expresses doubts that the advances of the nineteenth century could be equaled.

(Chippewa Falls) Daily Independent, January 8, 1901

What is the present outlook for the twentieth century? This question is variously answered, but the answer of the most eminent prophets, whether orthodox or heterodox, Christian or agnostic, is pessimistic rather than optimistic, whether the critic speaks from the standpoint of Europe or America. Bishop Potter, in America, looks forward to an increased sway of Materialism, the greed of wealth whose baleful increasing influence he sees in the college, the church, in the market place, in the shop, in society, high and low. Rev. Dr. John Watson (Ian Maclure) fears that while the people are now the rulers, have better wages, more decent hours and ample means of education, they have no strong spiritual life, do not know how to use their votes, have not learned to be frugal and temperate, read great books without thinking about the great questions. In short, Dr. Watson believes that the people

"Old Father Time—'What! Two of you this time!'"
Stevens Point Journal, *December 31, 1900 and*

have grown careless and frivolous with freedom and prosperity, and that their gods are pleasure and comfort. . . . He finds the blight of commonplace settling down on the church. He finds but very few men of genius and eloquence in the pulpit. He finds intelligence, education, clever, cheap work in literature and the pulpit, but it is the excellence of uniformity, the average man coming into his kingdom.

Same Old World or Glorious Century?

> The turn of the century was a time for reflecting on the old and the new. Newspapers, speeches, and sermons devoted attention to the future and offered widely differing perspectives. The final two pieces recognize that the turning of the century was no more important than any other day, and yet found the day an opportune moment for reflection. Whether it would be "the same old world" or a "glorious century" was too appealing a question to ignore.

(Chippewa Falls) Weekly Herald, January 4, 1901

The Nineteenth Century passes away into history to-night. In history it will hold a commanding place. The things which have come to pass within the sweep of the hundred years have been of immense proportions. Man has become master of more of the elements of life than were dreamed of at the birth of the century and progress in all lines has been on a grand scale. Human life has been made more worth having and humanity has much to be thankful for. Conjecture as to what the new century has in store for the world is great, of course, and many predictions of optimistic, as well as pessimistic shades, are advanced. But it seems doubtful that the next century will show any greater progress than has the past. Of course men have gained in wisdom and have learned many new ways to apply that wisdom, but nevertheless it is hardly probable that the progress of the new will surpass that of the old century.

Periods of great prosperity are followed by periods of depression and, in the same way, a spurt of advancement is sure to be followed by a relaxation. The world will be no better because of passing the century mile-post. The affairs of men will continue to be tangled in the web of human misunderstanding and wars will be fought, while churches will grow with the growth of population, in the same ratio that the number of thieves and evil-inclined people will increase.

It will be the same old world, with the difference that the letter-heads will be dated 1901, up to 2000.

Kenosha Evening News, December 29, 1900

It was Charles Lamb who wrote, "of all sounds of bells most solemn and touching is the peal which rings out the old year." Much more is this true when the knell of the century is sounded. The last day of this December marks an event which ought to sober every mind with a sense of the august flight of time and quicken every heart with a feeling of the brotherhood of man, yet it may well excite as much joy and happy anticipation as of solemnity and sober misgiving.

We approach the dawn of the new century with none of superstitious expectations of portent or judgment with which the world approached the dawn of the tenth century and with none of the flippant "after us the deluge" cynicism with which it approached the dawn of the nineteenth. What the twentieth shall contain for good or ill for mankind only the passing years can reveal—whether it shall be a Pandora's box out of which shall come hatred, war, pestilence, famine, greed of gain and unbridled ambition, or whether it shall be under the spell of a good fairy dispensing peace, plenty, joy and good will among men and nations. The pessimist is not likely to see the former wholly prevail, nor can the optimist hope to see all the latter realized. As has been the experience of the past, the world is likely to get a share of both good and ill, and the conditions will in large measure be of mankind's own making and choosing.

All things considered, this old world, wicked as it is, is a vastly better place to live in at the close of the nineteenth century than it was at its beginning, and it is a reasonable assumption that it will be a still more desirable place of residence at the close of the twentieth century than it is at its beginning, though none of us will be here to tell whether it is or not. At all events it is better and more comfortable to take a roseate view of the new century—to welcome it with hope and joy and yet with reverence. If it shall bring such marvelous developments as has the closing century, it will be a wonderful epoch in the world's history. No seer can foresee the possibilities which the oncoming 100 years may hold for mankind. If righteousness and justice and brotherly love shall go hand in hand with the advance of science, with the dissemination of knowledge and the development of nature's resources, then indeed it will be a glorious century.

Suggestions for Further Reading

Although the literature on the observance of new centuries is not extensive, there are a number of intriguing works for those who wish to explore the way people celebrated and thought about the opening of the twentieth and other centuries. A fascinating book that covers the way new centuries were observed over a millennium is Hillel Schwartz, *Century's End: A Cultural History of the Fin de Siècle from the 990s through the 1990s* (New York, 1990). Peter Stearns presents his study, *Millennium III, Century XXI: A Retrospective on the Future* (Boulder, 1996), as a handbook for understanding millennial hype, but also offers a good historical background on century celebrations and the development of the Christian calendar. Another recent title that covers similar ground from a different perspective is Stephen Jay Gould, *Questioning the Millennium: A Rationalist's Guide to a Precisely Arbitrary Countdown* (New York, 1997). For an interesting discussion of the development of methods of tracking the passage of time, see David Ewing Duncan, *Calendar: Humanity's Epic Struggle to Determine a True and Accurate Year* (New York, 1998).

Readers who are interested in learning more about Wisconsin at the turn of the century should consult John D. Buenker, *The History of Wisconsin. Volume IV: The Progressive Era, 1893–1914* (Madison, 1998). For an overview of the nation at the approach of the new century, see David Traxel, *1898: The Birth of the American Century* (New York, 1998) and Judy Crichton, *America 1900: The Turning Point* (New York, 1998). Crichton's book is the companion volume for the film *America 1900,* which was originally broadcast as part of a PBS television series, *The American Experience.*

There is no better way to get a feel for the late nineteenth century's view of the future than by reading the literature of the time. The best place to start is Edward Bellamy's, *Looking Backward, 2000–1887,* published in 1888 and still available in good editions.

Index